10 SECRETS TO ACING ANY HIGH SCHOOL TEST

10 SECRETS TO ACING ANY HIGH SCHOOL TEST

Lee Brainerd

AND

Ricki Winegardner

NEW YORK

Library of Congress Cataloging-in-Publication Data:
Brainerd, Lee Wherry.
    10 secrets to acing any high school test / Lee Brainerd and Ricki Winegardner—
2nd ed.
        p. cm.
Includes bibliographical references.
    ISBN 1-57685-437-X (pbbk.)
    1. Test-taking skills. 2. Examinations—Study guides. 3. Study
skills. I. Title: Ten secrets to acing any high school test. II. Winegardner,
Ricki. III. Title.
    LB3060.57.B73 2003
    371.3'028'1—dc21

                                                      2002152872

Printed in the United States of America
9 8 7 6 5 4 3 2 1
Second Edition

ISBN 1-57685-437-X

For more information or to place an order, contact LearningExpress at:
    900 Broadway
    Suite 604
    New York, NY 10003

Or visit us at:
    www.learnatest.com

ABOUT THE AUTHORS

Lee Wherry Brainerd is the author of *Basic Skills for Homeschooling* and *Homeschooling Your Gifted Child*, and has edited and contributed to many books on topics ranging from healthcare to test preparation. She lives in Altadena, California.

Ricki Winegardner is the author of *A Parent's Guide to 3rd Grade* and *A Parent's Guide to 4th Grade*, and coauthor of *Basic Skills for Homeschooling*. She is a producer for AmericanBaby.com and lives in McConnellsburg, Pennsylvania.

CONTENTS

INTRODUCTION

Your palms are sweaty, your stomach is in a knot, and you think you feel a headache coming on. You even thought about staying in bed today instead of going to school. No, you don't have the flu; you are simply on your way to take a test for which you feel ill-prepared. Fortunately, your symptoms can be cured! Mix some preparation with a few time management skills, wash it all down with a healthy mind and body, and, voila, you will feel better about test taking in no time!

As a high school student, your days may seem to be filled with these small inconveniences referred to as tests. A pop quiz in one class leads into a major chapter test in another. Then, after you have gotten into the routine of school test taking, you will be presented with standardized testing. Standardized tests are used by educational institutions and lawmakers to gauge the overall proficiency of students in a given school or geographical region. Perhaps the monsters of all tests are the college entrance exams that you have heard so much about. Examples of college entry exams include the Scholastic Aptitude Test (SAT) exam and the ACT Assessment. You are even required to take tests to enter the military or drive a car. During these high school years, it seems that tests are becoming more than a fact of life; they are slowly taking over many facets of your everyday existence. In truth, tests are a fact of life, and if you lack the proper test-taking skills, life can be difficult.

This book is designed to help you gain control over test stress and to provide you with the skills necessary to become a more successful and confident test taker. The ten secrets to taming even the most daunting and stressful of tests will be revealed to you in ten easy-to-reference chapters.

Secret #1: Managing Time and Being Prepared

Time management is a skill that is referred to even in the corporate world. Gone are the lazy days of childhood when morning melted into afternoon, which somehow oozed into evening. As you and your responsibility load have grown, so have the expectations that you will learn to manage your time effectively. Early lessons in time management can be traced back to when you were assigned a chore to be completed after school but before dinner. Maybe you came home and unloaded the dishwasher immediately, or perhaps you waited until the last possible moment before the food was placed on the table. In either case, you were given a task and a block of time in which to perform that task, and it was up to you to make decisions about how you would manage your time.

Effective time management will greatly reduce the stress you feel when walking into the classroom on test day. If you have used your time effectively, you will have studied and prepared yourself without undue stress.

The skill that goes hand in hand with time management is preparation. No matter how efficient you are at managing your time, you will have difficulty overcoming hurdles if you are not prepared. Preparation means creating weekly study schedules to maximize your time. Preparation means that you have your #2 pencil with you, if required. Preparation means that you possess a basic idea of what to expect on the test, and it also means that you are always ready for the pop quizzes for which your science teacher has become famous. Effectively managing your time to prepare for an exam is half the battle to becoming a more successful and confident test taker. For this reason, Secret #1 pairs both time management and preparedness together.

Secret #2: Getting a Handle on Objective Testing

Several types of test will be administered to you during your high school and post-high school career. You have probably already been exposed to most, if not all, of the major styles of testing. When asked which kind of test you prefer, you and many of your friends may answer that you prefer objective tests. Examples of objective test questions include:

- multiple choice
- true or false

- fill-in-the-blank
- sentence completion

Objective tests are often favorites among students because what the teacher is looking for is very clear to them. On an objective test, you may be presented with a question and then be expected to choose from a list of possible answers. Of course, at least one of these answers is the correct answer to the presented problem. The answer is either correct or incorrect, with no concern for instructor or tester opinion.

Other objective tests provide you with clues to a correct answer and then require that you provide the answer on your own. You may need to fill in a blank or complete a phrase or sentence. There are advantages and disadvantages to each type of objective test question. You can learn more about getting a handle on objective testing by turning to Secret #2.

Secret #3: Getting a Handle on Subjective Testing

Whereas objective testing typically requires that the test taker provide the specific answer for which the test maker is looking, subjective testing is a bit more reliant upon opinion. Examples of subjective test components include:

- essay questions
- short answer
- rubrics

When taking a subjective test, you may be expected to write essays, to provide well thought-out answers to problems that are presented, or to provide opinion along with facts and statistics to support your answer or opinion.

Other types of subjective tests may require you to fulfill a given set of requirements that may or may not be related to the answer you are providing. These types of tests are based on *rubrics*. When taking a rubric test in English class, you may be asked to write an essay entitled "The Hazards of Alcohol Abuse." Although it is important that you present a factual and well thought-out answer, the instructor may be grading on grammar, spelling, and sentence variation. Typically, when taking a rubric exam, the student is familiar with the requirements that need to be met to obtain a high score. It is up to you, the student, to be sure to meet the required elements of the rubric guidelines to obtain the score you desire. Tips for getting a handle on subjective tests can be found in Secret #3.

Secret #4: Mastering Your Study Environment

Where, when, and how you study are all very important factors in your overall test performance. By now, you may have an idea of what type of study environment works best for you. Do you learn best when studying with others, combining studying with socializing, or do you do your best when studying alone in a quiet corner of the house? Learning how to take control of your study environment will increase your odds for test success. Secret #4 offers you all the advice you need to succeed.

Secret #5: Discovering Your Learning Style

Studies have shown that there are many different learning styles and methods. Sitting alone in a quiet room in front of a book may work for one student but not for another. Do not force yourself to study in a certain way just because it is generally considered the best way. Learn what works best for you. Do you study better in a group or alone? Is simply reading the textbook enough for you, or does listening to a lecture that you taped in class help you the most? The most advantageous way to study is by using the methods that best fit your learning style. If you are not sure of your learning style and how to tailor your study habits to that style, turn to Secret #5.

Secret #6: Creating and Implementing a Study Plan

Instead of flying by the seat of your pants for your high-stakes exams, create a study plan, implement it, and discover that studying becomes a non-intrusive part of your everyday lifestyle.

For many students, the thought of preparing for a very important test sends them into panic mode. Some students' solution is to actually avoid studying during the months prior to test time and cram the final week before the BIG TEST. But you're not one of those students, right? You got this book to help you prepare and use a study plan to get the scores you know you can earn, given the right preparation. Learn all about making your study plan in Secret #6.

Secret #7: Getting the Most Out of Class

Some of your best study time may be during school hours. What better way to manage your time than to make the time you spend in the classroom benefit you the most? Use your time in class to prepare for the test by being attentive, knowing when and how to ask questions, and, of course, learning to take effective notes. Class time turns into study time in Secret #7.

Secret #8: Mastering the Materials

This may seem obvious, but mastering the materials that will be covered on an exam is key to good test performance. You will not perform up to par on an exam if you have not mastered the material that is to be covered. Secret #8 uncovers the tips to effectively learning the facts and materials that are covered in class. You will learn how to study in small bites rather than in large chunks and how to optimize class time by learning to listen to the teacher and picking out key words and phrases that will be on the tests while also honing your note-taking skills. Did you know that your homework assignments are often windows to the upcoming test? It's true! Teachers often create tests from previously assigned homework assignments. Learn these strategies and more in Secret #8.

Secret #9: Tackling Memory Tricks

Those who perform well on tests often have tricks to help them remember important information. Word games, fact association, and other memory tricks and skills are covered, or shall we say uncovered, in this chapter! Learn to use mnemonics, acronyms, acrostics, and peg and place methods to memorize vocabulary, formulas, and much more.

Secret #10: Preventing Test Stress

Just as with any major event in life, stress can play a detrimental role in test taking. Combine the previous nine secrets to overcome and prevent test stress. There are other stress factors that can affect your ability to succeed on a test, including family problems, peer pressure, low self-esteem, and many others. Recognize those stresses in your life that detrimentally affect your study habits and test taking. Actively work to alleviate these stresses. Once the stress is alleviated, you will be able to walk into the testing room more confident and relaxed. Helpful tips for minimizing test stress can be found in Secret #10.

How to Use This Book

At the beginning of each chapter, you will be introduced to a student or students. These high school teens are just like you in that they are seeking ways to improve or hone their study and test-taking skills.

You will not improve your grades and become a more confident and able test taker simply by owning this book. This book is most helpful when it is used to plan a full strategy for more successful test taking. Uncover the 10 Secrets one by one, and then use them to formulate the best plan for you. Also, refer back to the book whenever you are faced with a particularly daunting or stressful test situation.

At the end of the book, you will also find a selection of resources gathered to allow you to strengthen your test-taking skills. These resources include:

- a guide to high school exams by state
- print resources
- online resources

Good luck!

10 SECRETS TO ACING ANY HIGH SCHOOL TEST

MANAGING TIME AND BEING PREPARED

Tyrone felt like he was the butt of an unfunny joke. His favorite teacher, Ms. Kariotis, was suddenly beginning her maternity leave early. That moved his chemistry final to next Tuesday, the same day as his Spanish final. "What's the good of scheduling," he asked his mother, "if the schedule always changes?"

The truth was that Tyrone was new to study plans and anxious about reprioritizing. Fortunately, the process of creating the first schedule made it much easier for him to create a second, and once he began reprioritizing, he discovered that most of his original study plan remained the same. He recognized that Sunday and Monday nights would be the crunch. He would have to leave Sunday's picnic early to begin reviewing his Spanish. Monday night he would have to start studying right after school. If he finished half of his chemistry review before dinner and half after, he would have the rest of Monday evening for Spanish, the subject he found more difficult. Tyrone wrote his new schedule for Sunday and Monday on his desk calendar.

Tyrone decided he liked the idea of breaking his work into chunks. That way meeting his goals didn't feel so overwhelming. Consequently, he scheduled a ten-minute telephone call to a friend once he had finished one half of his Spanish review. After a moment, Tyrone crossed out the *10* and replaced it with *20 only*. He couldn't think of a friend who would only talk for ten minutes.

Like Tyrone, you can learn how to reprioritize your schedule when unexpected changes and events arise. Time management is a skill that requires practice, but after a while, it will become second nature. In this chapter, you will learn how to manage your study time and prepare both mentally and physically for exams.

WHAT IS TIME MANAGEMENT?

Time management is a skill that you will use your whole life. You will either be very good at managing your time, very poor at managing your time, or somewhere in the middle. Time management is used to describe the skill of effectively organizing and utilizing your time to best complete your tasks and responsibilities. This skill takes time to perfect, but if you begin by learning some of the basics of time management, as well as some tricks that you can use to help you become a better time organizer, you will soon find the time management techniques that work for you.

When we think of time management, we usually envision wooden building blocks. There are many different sizes of building blocks. Small blocks represent the small tasks in life, the ones that can be completed in a short period of time. Larger blocks represent the more ominous tasks or responsibilities. Once you have assigned each task to an appropriately sized block, you just need to fit these blocks together so that they do not topple—so that they are manageable.

SOURCES IN CYBERSPACE

Time Management
- www.gmu.edu/gmu/personal/time.html—Tips and strategies for effective time management.
- www.bigchalk.com—Tips and strategies for effective time management in high school.
- www.makingitcount.com/HighSchool/gettingthegrades/—Time management tips.

TIME AND THE TEENAGER

As a teenager, you may understandably have a very busy schedule. This is especially true if you are involved in extracurricular activities, sports, or community organizations, or if you have a part time job. You may also have family obligations, such as tending to younger siblings after school or chipping in with some of the household chores. In addition to all of these obligations, you probably have an active social life, including a core group of friends and possibly social events such as dances and evenings at the mall. When you look at your collection of time blocks, you may very well feel overwhelmed. All of these things are important to you and to your social and emotional growth, but unfortunately, if not managed correctly, any or all of them may have a detrimental effect on your test scores. Learning to manage your time effectively can only enhance all of these aspects of your life. You will find that the better you manage your time, the more time you will have for the things you enjoy doing, such as going to the movies.

Let's face it: There are going to be times that you will be tempted to use your study time for other less productive activities. These temptations will follow you throughout your life. If you are an effective time manager, you will learn to either resist them or to effectively juggle your schedule so that you can take part in the more tempting activity, while rescheduling and actually doing the activity that you had originally scheduled. You may also, when organizing your time, build your schedule with some padding so that you will be able to deal with unexpected events or temptations when they occur.

MANAGE YOUR TIME EFFECTIVELY

When we talk about time management in this chapter, we are going to discuss it in two different contexts. First, we will talk about how to manage your time during the days and hours leading up to a test, and then we will discuss how to best manage your time while actually taking the test. Sprinkled throughout the chapter are tips for being prepared for whatever test comes your way, whether it is the pop quiz or the state-required standardized test. Learning to utilize your time effectively both before and during a test can have nothing but positive effects on your test results.

Before the Test

Time management before the test encompasses the days and even weeks leading up to the exam. Learning how to effectively organize yourself and your activities during your out-of-school hours is extremely important. As mentioned previously in this chapter, teenagers tend to be very busy, and most of the activities that keep them busy are not taking place during the normal school day. These activities take place before and after school and on weekends. That is why it is imperative to gain the skills necessary to manage all of your time—the hours that you are in school as well as the hours that you are not.

The first step to gaining control of your time is to get a handle on exactly how much you do each week. Figure out how much of your time is scheduled *for* you compared to how much time *you* actually control. This can be accomplished by creating a series of schedules.

- **Long-term schedule**
  Make a list of your weekly obligations. This list can include items such as work schedule, classes, sports practices, and religious services. Be sure to include all of your recurring weekly obligations on this schedule. You will only need to make this schedule once but should modify it when necessary.

  Tyrone's long-term schedule looks like this:

Sunday	10:00 A.M.–12:00 P.M.: Church 1:00 P.M.–3:00 P.M.: Family picnic
Monday	8:00 A.M.–4:00 P.M.: Classes 4:30 P.M.–6:30 P.M.: Swim practice
Tuesday	8:00 A.M.–4:00 P.M.: Classes 4:30 P.M.–6:30 P.M.: Swim practice 7:00 P.M.–9:00 P.M.: Work at Jay's Pizza
Wednesday	8:00 A.M.–4:00 P.M.: Classes 4:30 P.M.–6:30 P.M.: Swim practice
Thursday	8:00 A.M.–4:00 P.M.: Classes 4:30 P.M.–6:30 P.M.: Swim practice
Friday	8:00 A.M.–4:00 P.M.: Classes 5:00 P.M.–7:00 P.M.: Work at Jay's Pizza
Saturday	9:00 A.M.–1:00 P.M.: Swim meets

- **Medium-term schedule**
  Make a list of your major weekly events. This list can include how much work you intend to complete in a given subject, any major social events you would like to attend, and any major school-related events, such as a weekly vocabulary test or the day a major paper is

due in English class. Ideally, you will create this schedule once a week. At the end of the week, review the schedule to see how many of your weekly tasks you were able to complete successfully. Always make a new list for each week. Do not reuse your weekly schedule.

Tyrone's medium-term schedule may look something like this:

Sunday	Study for Spanish final
Monday	Study for Spanish final Study for chemistry final
Tuesday	Take Spanish final Take chemistry final
Wednesday	Start reading *The Hobbit*
Thursday	Complete Chapters 3 and 4 of *The Hobbit* by Friday
Friday	See movie with Shane
Saturday	Attend swim meets

- **Short-term schedule**

Make a list of your daily events. On a 3 x 5 index card, write down the important activities and assignments for the day. This card should be easy for you to carry with you. The schedule should be created daily, perhaps before bedtime or in the morning during breakfast.

Tyrone created a short-term schedule for Monday that looked something like this:

- 7:00 A.M.–7:20 A.M. Mental review of Spanish while eating breakfast
- 1:30 P.M.–2:10 P.M. Study for chemistry final in study hall
- 4:00 P.M.–4:25 P.M. Study for chemistry final
- 4:30 P.M.–6:30 P.M. Swim practice
- 6:30 P.M.–7:00 P.M. Review Spanish verbs on the way home from practice with Mom
- 7:15 P.M.–7:45 P.M. Dinner and family time
- 7:45 P.M.–8:30 P.M. Study for chemistry final
- 8:30 P.M.–8:50 P.M. REWARD! Call a friend and have a snack
- 8:50 P.M.–9:30 P.M. Study for Spanish final

It is very important that you carry this card with you at all times. Cross off each item as it is completed. You will undoubtedly feel a sense of accomplishment every time you cross one of your tasks off your list. Also, writing down tasks forces you to really think about what you need to accomplish in a day, fills you with a sense of responsibility to stick to the plan, and shows you the types of tasks that you put off until the last minute. Notice that Tyrone built things into his schedule such as practice, a snack, and a phone call with a friend. Be sure to include these items in your schedule. Taking breaks, exercising, and eating well are all keys to successful studying.

True mastery of knowledge does not happen with an overnight cram session. The only way to truly learn a subject is to learn it bit by bit over time. For that reason, it is important that you begin studying for a test the first day that material is introduced. Spend a little time every day recalling key ideas and facts from each of your classes.

STUDY AEROBICS

Benefits of Multitasking

Get more accomplished by combining two or more activities into one. If you can do two things at once, like rub your stomach and pat your head, try applying this strategy to your time management problems and plan. If, for example, you have chores to do but also need to study, combine the two activities. Record vocabulary words and their definitions onto a cassette tape and play it as you wash the dishes or clean your room. Instead of reading magazines, flip through flashcards while you are waiting for your dentist or doctor's appointment.

During the Test

Just as important as managing your time appropriately before a test is the skill of managing every minute of your time during the actual test. Few tests have absolutely no time constraints on them. Even if the test you are taking is not a timed standardized test, there is usually the expectation that you will complete the test in a given period of time.

You may be expected, for instance, to complete the test during one class period.

Because you have a basic idea of how much time you have, you can make some decisions about how you will proceed when taking the test. There are certain guidelines that may help you allot and manage your time while taking a test.

- **Pay attention to the number of points each question is worth and allot your time accordingly.**

  It is not uncommon for questions on tests to have different point values assigned to them. A set of true or false questions may be worth two points each, whereas an essay question may be worth ten points. Before answering any of the questions, look over the test to see if there are some questions that are worth more points than others.

- **If you have trouble with a question, go on to the next one and come back to it later, if possible.**

  Do not spend too much time on any one question. Remember how much time you allotted yourself for each question, and do your best to stay within your guidelines. If a question has you stumped, mark it with your pencil or make a note of it on scrap paper, and return to it after you have completed all the other questions on the test.

- **Make brief, concise notes for each essay question.**

  Before providing a detailed answer to an essay question, make short, meaningful notes about the items you would like to cover in your answer. This serves two purposes. The first is to get all of your thoughts down quickly so that you will have all of the pieces necessary to answer the question completely. The second is that if, for some reason, you are unable to come back to the question, you will have at least provided an answer. Sure, the answer may not be as complete as you intended, but you may still earn partial credit.

BE PREPARED!

What is the first thing you think of when you hear the statement "Be prepared"? After recognizing it as the motto of a well-known scouting organization, do you think of being mentally, physically, or functionally prepared for your exams?

Mental Preparation

Mental preparation refers not only to studying and reviewing content and subject matter to gain a thorough understanding of the material to be covered in the test; it also refers to the state of mind that you are in when you walk into the testing room, as well as your mental well-being during the testing process.

If you have listened carefully in class, spent time every day reading and reviewing class materials and resources, and asked the instructor for clarifications on any concepts that you may not have fully under-stood, then you already have taken a huge step in ensuring that you are mentally prepared for your exam.

It is also important that you try to alleviate any stress in your life that could impact your performance on the exam. Be sure to arrive for the test on time. Do not over schedule yourself on the day of an important test. Manage your time effectively so that time is not a stress causer but a stress reliever.

Before the test, take a minute to think positive thoughts. Surround yourself with positive-minded friends who are supportive and will help you feel comfortable and confident on test day.

Physical Preparation

Unless your test is in a class such as physical education, you may think that physical preparation is not an important part of taking an aca-demic test. The truth is that in order to succeed, you must have both a healthy mind and a healthy body.

Be sure that you get plenty of sleep the night before a test. Ideally, you should be aware of your sleeping habits even on days when you don't have tests because lack of sleep may greatly diminish your abil-ity to concentrate and retain information. The less effective you are at retaining information on a daily basis, the more you are going to have to cram before tests. Be sure that you are well rested on test day so that your mind is at its sharpest!

Food for thought—be sure that you eat a well balanced breakfast on test day. Studies have shown that eating a healthy breakfast enhances a student's proficiency in school. Even if you are pressed for time, take a minute to eat breakfast. If your test is not until after lunchtime, think about what you are eating for lunch. Try to stay away from heavy meals that will make you feel tired. Although it is important that your body have the food it needs for brainpower, you should not overeat either!

Try to dress appropriately for the test environment. Dress comfortably, ensuring that none of your clothing becomes a distraction to you or others during the test. Test day is not the day to wear clothes that are too tight, too loose, or too loud. You want to focus all of your brainpower on answering questions, not on thinking about how uncomfortable you are. In addition, consider whether or not the testing room is air-conditioned. Will you need to take a sweater? Will you be overheated? Are you allowed to take bottled water into the room with you?

Functional Preparation

Do you have a number two pencil? This question is an example of functional preparation. Do you have what you need or are required to have in order to take this test? Some tests require that you register ahead of time. Have you preregistered? The instructor may have said that she will allow you to use your notebooks for this test. If so, have you remembered your notebook? You see that functional preparation refers to the items and processes that must occur for you to take the test. You may have studied voraciously and you may be dressed appropriately, but if you are not functionally prepared for the test, it could all be for nothing!

MINDBENDER

Time Management Quiz

Do you often (Yes or No):

YES NO

_____ _____ 1. Feel that you don't have enough time to get everything done?

_____ _____ 2. Begin to study for an exam or work on an assignment and realize it's going to take twice as long as you thought?

_____ _____ 3. Feel like you're rushing all day long, jumping from one thing or place to another, yet never accomplish much?

_____ _____ 4. Spread yourself too thin, committing to more extracurricular and social activities than you can possibly handle?

_____ _____ 5. Finish big projects and papers the night before they're due?

_____ _____ 6. Feel as though you're running late?

_____ _____ 7. Feel that you never have any time to relax?

_____ _____ 8. Set goals that you never achieve?

_____ _____ 9. Procrastinate by putting off difficult assignments until the very last minute?

_____ _____ 10. Feel that you spend most of the day doing things you don't enjoy?

To see how well you manage your time, total the number of "yes's" and compare to the following:

Score
If your total number of Yes answers was

0—Great! You're organized and plan your time effectively. Well done!

1–3—You usually manage your time pretty well but may falter once in a while. You need to create a schedule you can stick to.

4–6—Your time management schedule is disorganized and out of control. Before you know it, activities and assignments are piling up so fast you can't keep track of them. You definitely need to organize your time more effectively.

7–10—It's time for you to learn some time management skills and take control of your life. This is one assignment for which you can't afford to procrastinate.

Adapted from West Central Technical College website: www.westcentral.org/academics/timemngt.pdf

IN SUMMARY

A large part of acing high school tests takes place before the tests even begin. Learning to manage your time efficiently and effectively, including taking the time to prepare your self physically, mentally, and functionally for the big test, will reap extraordinary rewards. See Secret #6 to learn how to create and implement a study plan. If you need help mentally and physically preparing yourself, you may want to take a look at Secret #10 for information on preventing test stress.

Just the Facts

- Take the time to prioritize your work.
- Create three types of schedules: long-term, medium-term, and short-term.
- Learn to manage your time both before and during the test.
- Be prepared mentally, physically, and functionally.

Secret 2

GETTING A HANDLE ON OBJECTIVE TESTING

Stephen went to the mall to buy a birthday present for his girlfriend. He took his friend Charlotte along to help because he always had a hard time making decisions. As they entered the mall, Charlotte asked him how he felt about the history test they had taken earlier in the day.

"Not so good," said Stephen. "It was multiple-choice." Stephen dreaded multiple-choice tests. After reading the question, he would read the answer choices three or four times, hoping that the right answer would jump out at him. But it rarely did. Every time he filled in an answer choice, he felt nervous and usually ended up changing his answer immediately after.

Charlotte, on the other hand, loved multiple-choice tests. "But multiple-choice questions are a cinch," she explained to Stephen. "The answer's right there. It's not like you have to pull it out of thin air."

"But I'd rather pull it out of thin air," he sighed. "I get distracted by all the choices."

Charlotte tried to cheer him up. "Well, next week we're having an essay exam in English. I'm sure you'll do well on that."

"Sure," Stephen said, "but what about the SAT? That's *entirely* multiple-choice."

Charlotte steers Stephen toward a jewelry store. "Don't worry so much," she said. After staring into a nearby jewelry case for a few moments, she looked up at him. "So," she said, "Do you want to get her a bracelet, a necklace, or earrings?"

"My whole life is one big multiple-choice test," he said, smiling despite himself.

"But it's just a present," Charlotte argued. "There's no right answer."

Stephen laughed. "You obviously don't know my girl-friend."

Like Stephen, many students have trouble scoring well on objective exams. However, a large number of the tests that you have taken throughout your school years and those that you will be taking in high school and beyond are classified as **objective tests.** Sometimes machine scored, these tests measure what you have learned with no regard to an outsider's opinion. On objective tests, your answers are either correct or incorrect. There is no middle ground or gray area. Mastering this type of test greatly improves your chances of becoming a successful test taker.

Objective tests typically contain questions in the following formats:

- multiple choice
- matching
- sentence completion
- true or false
- grid-in

Let's cover each of these types of questions in depth to uncover the secrets to mastering them.

MULTIPLE CHOICE

Although you may have heard multiple-choice exams referred to as "multiple guess," you can take the guesswork out of the equation if you have the proper skills. In this chapter, let's replace "guess" with "logical thinking." The typical multiple-choice question is made up of a sentence or a phrase called the "stem" and a list of three or four possible answers. One of the possible answers is the correct answer, and the others are often referred to as "distractors" or "decoys." As the names imply, the incorrect answers that surround the correct one are there to trick and confuse you. It will be up to you to logically decide which of the answers cannot possibly be correct, which may be correct, and which are the closest to being correct.

Examples

1. *Stanza* is to *poem* as
   a. *concerto* is to *symphony.*
   b. *portrait* is to *painting.*
   c. *hammer* is to *toolbox.*
   d. *volume* is to *encyclopedia.*
   e. *suit* is to *skirt.*

2. Which of the following words is synonymous with *mollify?*
   a. harden
   b. soften
   c. lengthen
   d. mold
   e. aggravate

3. By how much does the product of 8 and 25 exceed the product of 15 and 10?
   a. 25
   b. 50
   c. 75
   d. 100
   e. 125

4. An ice cream parlor makes a sundae using one of six different flavors of ice cream, one of three different flavors of syrup, and one of four different toppings. What is the total number of different sundaes that this ice cream parlor can make?
   a. 72
   b. 36
   c. 30
   d. 26
   e. 13

How did you do?

Answers

1. d. A *stanza* is a unit of a *poem*. A *volume* is a unit of an *encyclopedia*. This is a part-to-whole relationship.

2. b. To *mollify* means "to soften."

3. b. To figure out by what amount quantity A exceeds quantity B, calculate $A - B$:
$(8 \times 25) - (15 \times 10) = 200 - 150 = 50$.

4. a. The total number of different sundaes that the ice cream parlor can make is the number of different flavors of ice cream times the number of different flavors of syrup times the number of different toppings: $6 \times 3 \times 4 = 72$.

When taking a multiple-choice test, first find out if there is a penalty for answering a question incorrectly or if only correctly answered questions will be counted. If there is no penalty for incorrect answers, leaving a question unanswered automatically means that the answer will be marked incorrect, so it is important that you make a conscious effort to answer every question, even those for which you are unsure of the answer.

It may be easy to get stuck on one particular question. Deep down you know which of the options is the correct answer. It is right on the tip of your pencil, but for some reason you just cannot see it clearly. Instead of passing over this question, you tap your pencil, rub your forehead, and stare at the ceiling in hopes that the answer will jump out in front of you. Be aware when this happens. You do not want to spend too much time on any one question. Spread your time across all questions, leaving enough time to go back and revisit the ones you were less sure about.

Mark questions that you are unsure about with a small line so that they are easily found when you have time to go back and check your work. Sometimes when you revisit a question like this, after first being completely stumped, the answer will just roll off your pencil. Perhaps you were able to subconsciously think through the question while answering the remaining questions, or perhaps you were clued in by one of the other test questions. Remember to manage your time effectively when taking a multiple-choice test.

Be sure to fill in the answer sheet carefully. Perhaps a kind teacher or instructor would notice if you inadvertently skipped a number on the answer sheet, thus shifting all of the answers by one question, but usually these types of answer sheets are scored by machines. All too often students have been disappointed with their scores not because of incorrect answers, but because they filled in their answer sheets incorrectly. Always compare the number of the question to the answer number that you are filling in.

Tips for Answering Multiple-Choice Questions

- **Anticipate the answer.**
  Read the stem. Try answering the question in your head before you look at the choices. This gets your mind working in the right direction, and there should be a feeling of recognition when you see the correct option listed. Chances are good that if the answer you came up with in your head appears in the list of options, it is the right answer.

- **Consider ALL the answers.**
  Don't just mark the first answer that "looks good." Multiple-choice answers can be tricky, and often the list of possible answers will be worded in such a way that you will be tempted to choose the first answer that seems correct . When you do this, you may miss the better answer that is lower on the list. These "almost" answers are placed in the test by design and test not only your knowledge of the subject area, but also your attention to detail. Remember, they are called "distractors" and "decoys" for a reason!

- **Try rephrasing the question.**
  Sometimes rewording a question jogs your memory. This technique is especially helpful in tests created by teachers. The teacher, in creating the test, may have lifted sentences directly from the textbook and then reworded them slightly. When you rephrase the question, you may rephrase it into a sentence that you recognize from your note taking or that you have read in your textbook.

- **If you are unsure of the answer, first eliminate the wrong or unlikely choices.**
  First, eliminate any answer that you are positive is wrong. Next, look for any answer that seems out of place; it probably is. This pares down the list of possible choices, and increases the odds that your guess will be correct.

- **Look for the all-or-nothing words in the sentence.**
  These types of words are also called "qualifiers." Words such as *all, most, some, no, never, least, always, equal, maximum, greatest, not, less, mainly, highest, lowest, most nearly,* and *best* are all qualifiers. Be especially wary of totalitarian words like *all* or *nothing*. These words are key in a sentence because by changing them you can drastically change the meaning of the sentence.

- **Look to the middle with numbers.**
  If your set of choices is a range of numbers, choose mid-range numbers. For instance, if your choices included 20, 50, 75, 100, the correct answer would most likely be either 50 or 75. This is because teachers tend to add decoys that are both higher and lower than the correct answer when creating a list of decoys.

- **Understand and recognize balance phrasing.**
  Balance phrasing is when two of the choices echo each other. For instance, if the correct answer on a test is "made the citizens richer," it would not be uncommon for the answer "made the citizens poorer" to appear as a decoy. When researchers analyzed a wide range of teachers' tests, they found that the correct answer is often one of the phrases that has a parallel or "echoed" decoy item.

  It is safe to say that this is another example of human nature entering the test writing process. If you are unsure of the answer and you see balance phrasing in your list of options, choose one of the balanced phrases.

- **The Cs and Ds have it!**
  Although it is preferred that you never have to guess on a test and that you will be able to either recall or deduce the correct answers using good study habits and logical thinking skills, there are times that you may be stumped! If you are taking a multiple-choice test and are at your wit's end, and if an unanswered question counts as an incorrect answer, then you may want to choose either option C or option D from your list of decoys. Studies have shown that C or D is often the correct answer.

MATCHING

Matching questions are often found on vocabulary and language arts tests, but can be found on tests on any subject. An example of a matching test includes a list of vocabulary words along the left side of the sheet with a coordinating set of definitions in a second column along the right side of the paper. You are then asked to "match" each word to its proper definition.

Examples

1. Match the words on the left with their proper definitions on the right:

   a. mediocre   _____ **1.** inelegant
   b. gauche   _____ **2.** complete
   c. urbane   _____ **3.** average
   d. consummate   _____ **4.** elegant

2. Match the words on the left with their proper parts of speech on the right:

   a. the   _____ **1.** noun
   b. of   _____ **2.** adverb
   c. apple   _____ **3.** verb
   d. slowly   _____ **4.** article
   e. ran   _____ **5.** preposition

How did you do?

Answers

1. a—3, b—1, c—4, and d—2
2. a—4, b—5, c—1, d—2, and e—3

Tips for Answering Matching Questions

- **Find out whether each answer is used only once.**
  Sometimes a teacher will allow the same answer, usually found in the column on the right side of the page, to be used more than once. If the directions are not clear about this, be sure to ask the teacher or instructor. If each answer can only be used once and you are allowed to write on the test, cross out the letter after you have used it so that you can see what's left. If you are not allowed to write on the test but have a piece of scrap paper, write the answer letters or numbers on the scrap paper and cross them off there.

- **Read all the items in both columns before answering any question.**

  Knowing all of the possibilities before marking your answers will cut down on the amount of second-guessing and answer changing later. Read both columns first, and then begin to mark your answers. Also, being familiar with the full range of information being covered on the matching test will allow you to understand the context of the questions as they relate to the answers.

- **Answer the questions you know first.**

  There is no better way to build confidence than to start off with the questions for which you are sure of the answers. After you have familiarized yourself with the information in both columns, begin with the information that is most familiar to you. Again, if you are allowed, mark off each answer as you use it. If not, use a piece of scrap paper to keep track of the answers that you have already used.

STUDY AEROBICS

Test Yourself

When studying for a test with a friend, create your own practice multiple-choice, true or false, and fill-in-the-blank questions. The process of creating questions will not only help familiarize you with the material but will also give you insight into the logic and construction of objective tests. Make sure your practice questions are challenging enough to require serious thought. Create challenging multiple-choice questions by coming up with truly distracting "distractors" that make the correct answer less obvious. Create challenging true or false questions by coming up with statements that are *almost* true except for one important detail or *seemingly* false if read too quickly. Create challenging fill-in-the-blank questions by writing out complete sentences and then deleting a key word. When you and your friend have both finished creating your practice exams, exchange them, and see how well you do.

SENTENCE COMPLETION

In the first two types of objective test questions, you were given the answers. Now, we move to a type of question where you will be expected to provide the answer on your own. Sentence completion questions may be more stressful to you simply because you will be forced to recall information rather than to choose the best option that is provided to you.

When taking a test that includes sentence completion questions, it is helpful to think about what the instructor or teacher has in mind. Understanding the context of the sentence can be very helpful in leading you to the correct answer to fill in the blank. Because the instructor usually has a specific answer in mind when creating the fill-in-the-blank questions, sentence completion tests are still considered objective rather than subjective.

Examples

1. Scientific knowledge is usually _____, often resulting from years of hard work by numerous investigators.
   a. ponderous
   b. implacable
   c. precarious
   d. cumulative
   e. egregious

2. Even though _____ meals cause her digestive trouble, my grandmother insists on eating her food as _____ as possible.
   a. piquant/spicy
   b. foreign/often
   c. astringent/slowly
   d. cold/quickly
   e. purgative/daintily

3. The human body has _____ bones.

4. _____ created a cure for rabies.

How did you do?

Answers

1. **d.**
2. **a.**
3. **206.**
4. **Louis Pasteur.**

Tips for Answering Sentence Completion (Fill-in-the-Blank) Questions

- **If you don't know the exact answer, come as close as you can.**
  Even if you do not give the exact word that the teacher wants, you may come close enough to get partial credit.

- **Check the number of blanks.**
  If the test creator has left more than one blank, chances are that he or she is looking for more than one word. The converse cannot always be held true. A single blank may hold a multi-word answer.

- **Look for "a" or "an."**
  Knowing basic rules of grammar can help provide hints to the answer. For example, a word that starts with a vowel should follow the word "an" in a sentence, whereas a word that starts with a consonant should follow "a." Also, study the sentence to decide if the correct answer is singular or plural.

- **Test your answer.**
  After you choose an answer, read the entire sentence to yourself using your answer in the sentence. If the sentence sounds clumsy, you may have answered incorrectly. If the sentence sounds familiar, you should feel more confident.

TRUE OR FALSE

True or false questions usually give you the best odds of answering correctly, but they are often the trickiest of the objective test questions. It is very important that you take the time to read the question completely, understanding each piece of the sentence or sentences that make it up.

Examples

_____ 1. At the 1932 Democratic National Convention, Franklin D. Roosevelt, the 34th president of the United States, said "I pledge you, I pledge myself, to a new deal for the American people."

_____ 2. The 15th amendment to the Constitution prohibits federal or state governments from infringing on citizens' right to vote, regardless of their race, color, or previous condition of servitude.

How did you do?

Answers

1. **False.** The quote is, in fact, attributed to Franklin D. Roosevelt, but he was the 32nd president of the United States, not the 34th.

2. **True.**

Tips for Answering True or False Questions

- **Watch out for absolutes.**
  Look for absolutes or all-or-nothing words like *always, never,* and *entirely.* There are very few things in life that are always true or always false. Questions that contain these words are often false.

- **It's either all true or all false.**
  Be sure that all pieces of the statement are correct before marking an answer true. In the example, "Germany, a country in Asia, is home to the Autobahn," only part of the statement is true. Germany *is* home to the Autobahn, but it is *not* a country in Asia. If any part of the statement is wrong, the whole thing is false.

- **Don't overanalyze.**
  Read the statement as it is written, without adding any of your own thoughts or ideas to what appears on the test. Sometimes students who are already nervous about the test will overanalyze a true or false question. When they do this, they either answer the question incorrectly or confuse themselves further and end up wasting time. It is imperative that you read the statement exactly as it appears.

- **Know your teacher.**
  Ideally, you will never have to rely on this tip, but when it comes to true or false questions, it may help you to know your teacher. It has been shown on teacher-created tests and quizzes that teachers often create more of one type of question than another. Some teachers have shown patterns of creating more questions with false answers, whereas others have shown a tendency to create more with true answers. If possible, look over some of your past tests to predict your teacher's tendencies. If you are unsure of your teacher's patterns, it is best to guess "true," because more teachers have the tendency to create true answers than false.

GRID-IN

Grid-in questions are also referred to as *student-produced responses*. The SAT exam has 10 grid-in questions, and some state exit exams have this type of question as well. Basically, you will be asked to solve a variety of math problems and then fill in the correct numbered ovals on your answer sheet. Again, the key to success with these problems is to think through them logically; that's easier than it may seem to you right now.

Examples

1. Tia is buying a shirt that regularly sells for $36.00 but is now on sale for $23.40. By what percent of the regular price has this shirt been discounted?

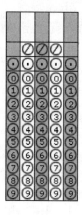

2. What is the next number in this sequence? Round your answer to the nearest thousandth. 8, 3.2, 1.28, 0.512, ___

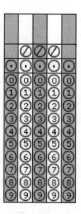

How did you do?

Answers

1. First, find the amount by which the price of the shirt has been reduced:

$$\$36.00 - \$23.40 = \$12.60$$

To find the percent of the reduction, divide the amount of the reduction by the original price:

$$\frac{\$12.60}{\$36.00} _____ = 0.35 = 35\%$$

2. Each term in the sequence is obtained by multiplying the preceding term by 0.4, so multiply the last term (0.512) by 0.4 to calculate the next term:

$$0.512 \times 0.4 = 0.2048$$

0.2048 rounded to the nearest thousandth is 0.205.

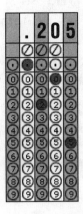

Tips for Answering Grid-In Questions

- **Write the answer in the column above the oval.**
  The answer you write will be completely disregarded because the scoring machine will only read the ovals. It is still important to write this answer, however, because it will help you check that you marked the appropriate ovals.

- **How to grid in your answer.**
  The answer grid can express whole numbers from 0 to 9999, as well as some fractions and decimals. To grid an answer, write it in the top row of the column and then fill in the appropriate ovals beneath each number. If you need to write a decimal point or a fraction bar, skip a column and fill in the necessary oval below it.

- **Answers that need fewer than four columns.**
  Answers that need fewer than four columns, except 0, may be started in any of the four columns, provided that the answer fits. If you are entering a decimal, do not begin with a 0. For example if you get 0.5 for an answer, simply enter .5.

- **If the answer fits the grid, do not change its form.**
  If you get a fraction that fits into the grid, do not waste time changing it to a decimal. Changing the form of an answer is completely unnecessary and can also result in a miscalculation.

- **Express mixed numbers as improper fractions or decimals.**
  As a math student, you are used to always simplifying answers to their lowest terms and converting improper fractions to mixed numbers. With grid-in questions, however, you should leave improper fractions as they are. For example, it is impossible to grid $1\frac{1}{2}$ in the answer grid, so simply grid in $\frac{3}{2}$ instead. You could also grid in its decimal form of 1.5. Either answer is correct.

- **Write fractions that require more than four digits as decimals instead.**
  The fraction $\frac{123}{175}$, for example, does not fit into the grid and it cannot be reduced; therefore, you must turn it into a decimal by dividing the numerator by the denominator. In this case, the decimal would be .70.

- **Use the most accurate value when entering decimals.**
  For example, if your solution is 0.333..., your gridded answer should be .333. A less precise answer, like .3 or .33, will be scored as an incorrect response.

- **Enter the decimal point and the first three digits of a long decimal.**
  If an answer is a repeating decimal, enter the decimal point and the first three digits of the decimal. Do not round the answer. It won't be marked wrong if you do, but it is a not necessary.

- **If a grid-in answer has more than one possibility, enter any possible answer.**
  This can occur when the answer is an inequality or the solution to a quadratic equation. For example, if the answer is $x < 5$, enter 4. If the answer is $x = + 3$, enter 3. There will not be any confusion because negative numbers cannot be entered into the grid.

- **Very important: Grid-in questions will not have negative answers.**
  If you get a negative number, you have done something wrong.

- **When entering percentages, grid the numerical value without the percent sign.**
  There is no way to grid the symbol, so it is not needed. For example, 54% should be gridded as .54. Don't forget the decimal point!

- **Be extremely careful.**
  The answer sheets are scored by a machine, so regardless of what else is written on the answer sheet, you will receive credit only if you have filled in the ovals correctly.
  Remember:

  1. If you write in the correct answer but do not fill in the oval, the question will be marked wrong.

  2. If you know the correct answer but fill in the wrong oval(s), the question will be marked wrong.

  3. If you do not fully erase an answer, it may be scored wrong. Be especially careful that a fraction bar or decimal point is not marked in the same column as a digit. Be sure to mark only one oval in each column.

Objective Testing

- www.xu.edu/lac/Objective_Tests.htm—Tips for taking objective tests.
- www.tulane.edu/~erc/studying/multiple.html—Tips for answering multiple choice questions.
- www.und.edu/dept/ULC/rf-objt.htm—Tips for answering all kinds of objective test questions.

MANAGING YOUR TIME DURING THE OBJECTIVE TEST

When taking an objective exam, you will want to pace yourself. Always use all of the test time allowed. If you complete the test, go back and check your answers. On an objective test, it is sometimes recommended that you work in three phases.

Phase I

Go through the entire test, answering only those questions that you are sure you can answer correctly. Skip all questions for which you are unsure of the answers. This is an especially important step for tests on which only answered questions are scored and those left blank are not counted. You have now ensured that you have a set number of correctly answered questions. Also, this gets the test going on the right foot! Instead of feeling defeated, you are filled with confidence as you move to Phase II.

Phase II

Review the test, looking only at the questions that you skipped in Phase I. This time, use some of the methods you have learned to eliminate trick or unlikely answers and decoys. When doing this, you should:

- identify and eliminate the answers that you know are definitely wrong or highly unlikely.

- eliminate those options that do not fit grammatically with the stem of a multiple-choice question.
- eliminate choices from the list of decoys that are redundant. Of the choices a) shouting, b) listening, c) staring, or d) yelling, choices a and d mean basically the same thing and because only one answer can be correct, it is logical that neither is the correct answer.

Phase III

If all else fails and you will be scored on all questions whether answered or not, it is time for you to use your logical thinking skills to make your best guess.

MINDBENDER

Your Guessing Ability

The following are ten really hard questions. You are not supposed to know the answers. Rather, this is an assessment of your ability to guess when you don't have a clue. Read each question carefully, just as if you did expect to answer it. If you have any knowledge about the subject of the question, use that knowledge to help you eliminate wrong answer choices.

Questions

1. September 7 is Independence Day in
   a. India.
   b. Costa Rica.
   c. Brazil.
   d. Australia.

2. Which of the following is the formula for determining the momentum of an object?
   a. $p = mv$
   b. $F = ma$
   c. $P = IV$
   d. $E = mc^2$

3. Because of the expansion of the universe, the stars and other celestial bodies are all moving away from each other. This phenomenon is known as
   a. Newton's first law.
   b. the big bang theory.
   c. gravitational collapse.
   d. Hubble flow.

4. American author Gertrude Stein was born in
   a. 1713.
   b. 1830.
   c. 1874.
   d. 1901.

5. Which of the following is NOT one of the Five Classics attributed to Confucius?
   a. the I Ching
   b. the Book of Holiness
   c. the Spring and Autumn Annals
   d. the Book of History

6. The religious and philosophical doctrine that holds that the universe is constantly in a struggle between good and evil is known as
   a. Pelagianism.
   b. Manichaeanism.
   c. neo-Hegelianism.
   d. Epicureanism.

7. The third Chief Justice of the U.S. Supreme Court was
   a. John Blair.
   b. William Cushing.
   c. James Wilson.
   d. John Jay.

8. Which of the following is the poisonous part of a daffodil?
   a. the bulb
   b. the leaves
   c. the stem
   d. the flowers

9. The winner of the Masters golf tournament in 1953 was
   a. Sam Snead.
   b. Cary Middlecoff.

c. Arnold Palmer.

d. Ben Hogan.

10. The state with the highest per capita personal income in 1980 was

    a. Alaska.

    b. Connecticut.

    c. New York.

    d. Texas.

How did you do?

Answers

Check your answers against the correct answers listed below.

1. **c.**
2. **a.**
3. **d.**
4. **c.**
5. **b.**
6. **b.**
7. **b.**
8. **a.**
9. **d.**
10. **a.**

You may have simply gotten lucky and actually known the answer to one or two questions. In addition, your guessing was more successful if you were able to use the process of elimination on any of the questions. Maybe you didn't know who the third Chief Justice was (question 7), but you knew that John Jay was the first. In that case, you would have eliminated answer **d** and, therefore, improved your odds of guessing right from one in four to one in three.

According to probability, you should get $2\frac{1}{2}$ answers correct, so getting either two or three right would be average. If you got four or more right, you may be a really terrific guesser. If you got one or none right, you may be a really bad guesser.

Just the Facts

- Remember, when taking an objective test, the answers are clearly right or wrong.

- Be slow to change an answer; your first impulses are usually correct.
- When there is no penalty for wrong answers, always make educated guesses.
- Review past tests if possible to identify your teacher's trends or tendencies.

GETTING A HANDLE ON SUBJECTIVE TESTING

Gene, Nita, and Tomoyuki sat in a far corner of the school library and faced their day of reckoning.

Determined to do well on their Advanced Placement (AP) English test, the three classmates agreed to practice their essay-writing skills together. Nita downloaded sample AP English essay questions from the Internet. Then they chose a question asking for a comparison of two Robert Frost poems, and they each wrote a rough-draft essay. Today was the peer-review stage in which each study group member would read another's essay and critique it.

"Are we still going to be friends after this?" Tomoyuki asked half-seriously. Gene critiqued Tomoyuki's essay first. Tomoyuki became a little defensive when Gene began with how difficult it was for him to read Tomoyuki's handwriting. Gene also thought that Tomoyuki's essay focused on one poem, with little mention of the second. Nita found that Gene's essay seemed to make the same point several times and had no closing sentence. Tomoyuki thought Nita had a terrific thesis statement but lacked logical connections leading from one point to another.

"Combined, we're perfect," Gene joked.

Gene, Nita, and Tomoyuki formed different opinions of what they read, so how can subjectivity possibly determine a fair grade? As you can tell from their experience, subjective tests are generally more complex than objective ones. When taking subjective exams, you have to do more than just select the correct answer from among several choices: You have to create a concise, often original, answer in your own words. This chapter will help you understand the different types of subjective testing, what they test, and how to study for them.

THE PURPOSE OF SUBJECTIVE TESTING

In the previous chapter, objective testing and the types of questions you can expect to find on that type of test were discussed. The topic of this chapter is **subjective testing**. This type of test often causes more stress for students because the distinction between a right and wrong answer is not always as clear as in objective testing. Also, in the subjective test, students may be asked to expand their thoughts beyond the facts that were taught in class, and they may be expected to form their own opinions and then provide the statistics or facts to support them. Subjective tests are almost always graded by people, not machines, which means that human opinion enters into determining how right or wrong a response is.

So, what is subjective testing? Subjective exams may call for responses ranging from a paragraph to several pages in length, depending on what type of question is involved. Subjective testing evaluates not only how well a student has memorized and can recall facts and theories but often also requires that the student take the information that was learned in the classroom and expand on it. By using this form of test, the educator can assess not only how well students have learned facts but also how well they have learned theory.

The questions on a subjective test usually encourage the student to utilize a variety of skills, from critical thinking to creativity, from proper spelling to proper sentence structure. The student will often need to take pieces of information that were learned and meld them into a coherent and convincing answer. Because the student is asked to formulate an answer this way, the subjective test can be a bit more difficult to study for.

The three students in the opening vignette provide a perfect example of the scoring process behind subjective tests. Although all three of the students thought that they had done suitable work, each was able to point out the areas where the others were lacking or where they could improve. Of course, all of the feedback provided was opinion based on a set of criteria, but many of the opinions are likely to be shared by the person scoring the AP test.

DIFFERENT TYPES OF SUBJECTIVE TESTS

There are several different types of subjective test questions. As you advance in your high school career, you are likely to see more and more of these types of tests.

Essay

There is nothing that can cause a collective groan in the classroom more effectively than a teacher informing students that the next test is going to include an essay question. The mere possibility of essay questions can send students into a panic.

Fortunately, because you are going to be well prepared and confident after using this book, you will no longer be one of those students. Essay questions may never be one of your favorite testing methods, but as you uncover the secrets to mastering them, you will become more comfortable with them.

Tips for Mastering Essay Questions

Consider the following sample essay question: Personification is the technique wherein a nonhuman character is given human thoughts, feelings, and dialogue. Illustrate how this technique is used in your favorite novel or short story.

1. **Read the directions and all questions carefully.**
   As with any type of test, it is imperative that all directions are read carefully and completely. Pay special attention to the question that you are being asked to answer. Identify key words and statements. These are clues to the expected answer. If you are permitted, underline the key words so that you can remain focused on exactly what the question is asking. Try to rephrase the question in the topic sentence of your answer.

The key words in the sample essay question are underlined below:

Personification is the technique wherein a nonhuman character is given human thoughts, feelings, and dialogue. Illustrate how this technique is used in your favorite novel or short story.

2. Use your time wisely.

As with objective test questions, it is very important that you use your time wisely. After you have read all of the test questions, prioritize which you are going to answer first, then estimate how much time you are going to allot for each question. Try to answer the least taxing questions first, moving on to those that will require more in-depth thought. By the time you reach the questions that require more thought, you should be in a groove, and your thoughts will be flowing more freely.

3. Create a short outline.

Before beginning a lengthy, disorganized exposition of your thoughts, use the key words and phrases that you identified earlier to outline your answer. Write this brief outline in the margin of your page or on scrap paper. This outline will help you stick to the point, keep your answer concise, and save you a lot of erasing when you realize that you have gone off track. A well-organized answer will be easy for the instructor to read, and, therefore, easy for the instructor to score. Here's a sample outline:

I. Introduce personification and Kipling's "Rikki-Tikki-Tavi"

II. Rikki-Tikki-Tavi as a humanized mongoose

III. Personification and the archetype of good and evil

IV. Conclusion

4. Be concise.

For most essay questions, instructors are looking for particular answers or groups of answers. While they are judging if you answered correctly and effectively, they will be looking for certain facts when reviewing the answers. Be sure that you answer only the question that is asked. Be direct, address all of the keywords and phrases, and do not allow your answer to be too lengthy.

This passage is too wordy: The technique of personification is a literary device used in many novels and short stories by many writers. In the short story "Rikki-Tikki-Tavi" by the author Rudyard

Kipling, nonhuman animals are personified, and they are also given the ability to be able to speak to each other in English. The fact that they are able to speak to each other like human beings makes them seem more real.

This passage is concise: In Rudyard Kipling's short story "Rikki-Tikki-Tavi," garden animals are personified and given the ability to speak English. Their personification makes the characters easier to identify with because they behave like human beings.

5. **Know your vocabulary!**

There are undoubtedly certain words and terms unique to the subject matter of your essay. Don't forget to use these terms in your answer. For example, in the sample essay question provided, *personification* should be mentioned throughout your response to the question. This not only shows a mastery of facts but also an understanding of the context in which you are writing. Keep in mind that you should not throw these words into your essay in a careless manner just for the sake of including them; that could have the opposite effect, and you could actually be penalized.

6. **Support your answer with examples and facts.**

You should be prepared to include examples and facts in your answer, especially when writing the answer to a "What is your opinion?" type of essay question. The statement, "I don't think that people should drink and drive" is not going to get you an "A" until you support that statement with some of the facts that you learned in the classroom.

7. **Evaluate your response.**

After completing your answer, do a quick evaluation of your essay by asking yourself these questions:

1. Does the essay clearly answer the question?

2. Is the topic clearly presented? Is a topic statement enough for this essay, or is the essay long enough to require a topic paragraph?

3. Have I provided enough facts and examples to support the essay?

4. Does the essay flow from thought to thought?

5. Is there a strong concluding statement or paragraph?

6. If this is a written exam, is my handwriting legible?

If your answer to any of these questions is "no," go back and edit your work.

Sample Essay

Personification is a clever technique in which nonhuman characters are given human characteristics. When the author uses this technique, the reader is able to understand how an animal feels, what a tree is thinking, or even the most intimate thoughts of an old pair of sneakers! Rudyard Kipling's "Rikki-Tikki-Tavi" is one of my favorite short stories. In it, all of the animals are personified, which is crucial, because the protagonist is a mongoose.

Rikki-Tikki-Tavi is a small mongoose who nearly drowns after a flood sweeps him away from his home. A boy named Teddy finds the mongoose, and he and his mother nurse the animal back to health. Although Rikki never converses with his human family, he converses in plain English with the other animals in the garden. This technique gives the reader the opportunity to become deeply involved in a story that revolves around a nonhuman protagonist. Even though Rikki-Tikki is unable to converse with the humans in the story, the reader is able to understand his character and thoughts.

Throughout the story, Rikki-Tikki finds himself battling adversaries in the garden in an effort to save Teddy's family, and because Kipling uses personification, we are able to hear and understand Rikki-Tikki's thoughts, feelings, and motivations as he does so. For example, before he battles Nag, the evil male serpent, he is cautious and a bit nervous but refuses to show his fear to his enemy. Only the reader understands Rikki's character from this point of view.

"Rikki-Tikki-Tavi" follows the archetype of a story about the battle between good and evil. If we look closely at the plot, biblical themes are also apparent. Nag, the snake in the garden, is an allusion to the story of Adam and Eve. Personification was also crucial in that story because Eve might not have been tempted by the serpent if he hadn't been able to speak. Similarly, Rikki-Tikki's story is enhanced by his conversations with the other animals. The reader is able to identify with Rikki-Tikki's character and sometimes forget that he is a mongoose because he is given human characteristics.

In the end, Rudyard Kipling was clever enough to observe what occurs in nature, blending it with personification and creating a timeless story of good versus evil.

SOURCES IN CYBERSPACE

Essay Writing Tips

- www.collegeboard.com—Essay writing tips (Search for "essay writing tips.").
- www.geocities.com/SoHo/Atrium/1437—The five-paragraph essay.
- www.bigchalk.com—Homework Central, the writing process.

Short Response

Short response questions are like mini essay questions. Students are expected to provide a written answer to a question but usually only in a few sentences. In the short response question, there is no room for answer padding. The questions are usually to the point, and the responses are expected to be as well.

Adapted from *Life on the Mississippi* by Mark Twain

My father was a justice of the peace, and I supposed he possessed the power of life and death over all men and could hang anybody that offended him. This was distinction enough for me as a general thing; but the desire to be a steamboatman kept intruding, nevertheless. I first wanted to be a cabin-boy, so that I could come out with a white apron on and shake a table-cloth over the side, where all my old comrades could see me; later I thought I would rather be the deck-hand who stood on the end of the stage-plank with the coil of rope in his hand, because he was particularly conspicuous. But these were lonely daydreams—and they were too heavenly to be contemplated as real possibilities. By and by one of our boys went away. He was not heard of for a long time. At last he turned up as apprentice engineer or "striker" on a steamboat. This thing shook the bottom out of all my [former beliefs]. That boy had been notoriously worldly, and I just the reverse; yet he was exalted to this eminence, and I left in obscurity and misery. There was nothing generous about this fellow in his greatness. He would always manage to have a rusty bolt to scrub while his boat tarried at our town, and he would sit on the inside guard and scrub it, where we could all see him and envy him and loathe him. And whenever his boat was laid up he would come home and swell around the town in his blackest and greasiest clothes, so that nobody could help remembering that he was a steamboatman; and he used all sorts of steamboat technicalities in his talk, as if he were so used to them that he forgot that common people could not understand them. He would speak of the "labboard" side of a horse in an easy, natural way that would make one wish he was dead. And he was always talking about "St. Looy" like an old citizen; he would refer casually to occasions when he was "coming down Fourth Street" or when he was "passing by the Planter's House," or when there was a fire and he took a turn on the brakes of "the old big Missouri"; and then he would go on and lie about how many towns the size of ours were burned down there that day. Two or three of the boys had long been persons of consideration among us because they had been to St. Louis once and had a vague general knowledge of its wonders, but the day of their glory was over now. They lapsed into a humble silence, and learned to disappear when the ruthless "cub" engineer approached. This fellow had money, too, and hair oil. Also an ignorant silver watch and a showy brass watch chain. He wore a leather belt and used no suspenders. If ever a youth was cordially admired and hated by his comrades, this one was . . . When his boat blew up at last, it diffused a tranquil contentment among us such as we had not known for months. But when he came home the next week, alive, renowned, and appeared in church all battered up and bandaged, a shining hero, stared at and wondered over by everybody, it seemed to us that the partiality of Providence for an undeserving reptile had reached a point where it was open to criticism.

This creature's career could produce but one result, and it speedily followed. Boy after boy managed to get on the river. The minister's son became an engineer. The doctor's and the post-master's sons became "mud clerks"; the wholesale liquor dealer's son became a bar-keeper on a boat; four sons of the chief merchant, and two sons of the county judge, became pilots. Pilot was the grandest position of all. The pilot, even in those days of trivial wages, had a princely salary—from a hundred and fifty to two hundred and fifty dollars a month, and no board to pay. Two months of his wages would pay a preacher's salary for a year. Now some of us were left disconsolate. We could not get on the river—at least our parents would not let us.

So by and by I ran away . . .

Short Response Question

How do the narrator's future plans change after he sees the boy who got a job on a steamboat? Use details and information from the passage to support your answer.

1. **Read the question carefully to understand what it asks.**
   Does this seem repetitive? Good, then you shouldn't forget: When taking a test it is of the utmost importance that you carefully read all instructions and all questions.

2. **Identify key phrases and words.**
   Just as with the essay questions, you will find that underlining key words will often focus your attention. These key words will help you identify the type of information that should be included in

your answer. The key words in the short answer question are underlined below:

How do the narrator's future plans change after he sees the boy who got a job on a steamboat? Use details and information from the passage to support your answer.

3. **Answer the question.**
   Start your answer by creating a sentence from the key words you identified. This sentence should include your key words or phrases as well as your answer. This is essentially your one sentence answer to the question.

4. **Reinforce your answer.**
   If necessary or desired, add a second or third sentence to reinforce the one-sentence answer that you provided in the previous step. This will be a supporting sentence that will include, perhaps, an example, reason, or short explanation relating to the first question.

Sample Response

The narrator had often dreamed of working on a steamboat, but he never thought those dreams could really come true. However, after one boy in his town gets a job on a steamboat and returns to the town to show off, the narrator and his friends become so envious that they decide to follow the boy's example. The narrator is determined to go to work on the river, but his parents refuse to give their permission. As a result, he ends up running away to pursue his dream.

In this response, the writer uses specific examples from the story to explain the narrator's decision to run away from home to get a job on a steamboat. The writer's descriptions of the narrator's reactions to the boy who got a job on a steamboat are accurate and create a complete picture of the emotions that lead the narrator to change his future plans.

Remember, subjective tests can pop up in math class too! In these tests, the *method* used to determine the correct answer is equally important as determining the correct answer itself. Here are a few examples of short response math questions and their answers:

Problem

1. For the following problem, you will be required to use estimation strategies.

   Mr. Montoya owns a greenhouse. As a test for a new variety of plant he wants to grow, he planted 204 seeds. Of these, 98 seeds germinated.

   Based on the test, *estimate* how many seeds Mr. Montoya should expect to germinate if he plants 3,986 seeds. Show your work or explain in words.

Explanation

If the test ratio holds, the expected number of plants that will germinate from 3,986 seeds can be calculated using the ratio $\frac{98}{204}$. For estimating purposes, round these numbers as follows:

$98 = 100$

$204 = 200$

$3,986 = 4,000$

Let x be the number of seeds expected to germinate. Set up a ratio and solve:

$$\frac{100}{200} = \frac{x}{4,000}$$

$$\frac{1}{2} = \frac{x}{4,000}$$

$$x = 2,000$$

Based on the test, Mr. Montoya can estimate that about 2,000 of his 3,986 seeds will germinate.

The calculation process may also be explained in words, as follows: Round the number of seeds that germinated (100 seeds is reasonable) and the number of seeds that were planted (200 seeds is reasonable) in the test to estimate the fraction of seeds that germinated. Round the number of seeds planted to a number compatible with the fraction of seeds that germinated in the test (4,000 is most compatible). Multiply the rounded number of seeds planted by the estimated fraction of seeds that germinated.

Estimated number of seeds that will germinate: 2,000 seeds

Problem

2. Alicia is trying to decide which type of service to sign up for with an Internet provider. The basic service offered by this provider costs $7.95 per month plus $2.25 per hour spent online. The frequent user service offered by this provider costs $15.95 per month plus $0.75 per hour spent online.

Part A: Write a system of two equations that could be used to find the monthly cost for using each type of service. Let c represent the monthly cost and h represent the number of hours spent online.

Part B: Determine the type of service for which Alicia should sign up. Show your work and explain your thinking.

Explanation

Part A

The services have the following costs:

For basic service: $c = 7.95 + 2.25h$

For frequent-user service: $c = 15.95 + 0.75h$

Part B

The two services cost the same when $(7.95 + 2.25h) = (15.95 + 0.75h)$

Solve for h:

$$7.95 + 2.25h = 15.95 + 0.75h$$
$$2.25h - 0.75h = 15.95 - 7.95$$
$$1.5h = 8.0$$
$$h = \frac{8.0}{1.5} = 5.33 = 5\frac{1}{3} \text{ hours}$$

If h is less that $5\frac{1}{3}$ hours, then the frequent-user service is more economical. (Substitute the value 6 in each equation to compare the costs.) If h is greater than $5\frac{1}{3}$ hours, then the basic service is cheaper. (Substitute the value 5 in each equation to compare the costs.)

Rubrics

The rubric test is the subjective form of testing in which you are probably given the most control over your own grade. When taking a rubric exam, guidelines are typically communicated to you ahead of time, and it is up to you to meet the appropriate guidelines for the score you desire. If, when looking over the rubric guidelines, you decide that your goal is to score average or above, then you can identify exactly how much work you will need to do to gain that score. You will also know the skills you may need to improve in order to earn that score. Below is a sample rubric.

Extended-Response Rubric

SCORE	DESCRIPTION
4	The response indicates that the student has a **thorough understanding** of the reading concept embodied in the task. The student has provided a response that is accurate, complete, and fulfills all the requirements of the task. Necessary support and/or examples are included, and the information is clearly text-based.
3	The response indicates that the student has an **understanding** of the reading concept embodied in the task. The student has provided a response that is accurate and fulfills all the requirements of the task, but the required support and/or details are not complete or clearly text-based.
2	The response indicates that the student has a **partial understanding** of the reading concept embodied in the task. The student has provided a response that includes information that is essentially correct and text-based, but the information is too general or simplistic. Some of the support and/or examples and requirements of the task may be incomplete or omitted.
1	The response indicates that the student has a **very limited understanding** of the reading concept embodied in the task. The response is incomplete, may exhibit many flaws, and may not address all requirements of the task.
0	The response is **inaccurate**, confused and/or irrelevant, or the student has failed to respond to the task.

Rubric tests fall under the heading of subjective tests because it is up to another person's judgment to decide if you did indeed meet the requirements of the rubric. Remember the three friends from the beginning of the chapter who were critiquing each other's work. If using a rubric that included legible handwriting as one of the pieces of grading criteria, Tomoyuki may have spent a little more time to ensure that his handwriting was legible.

STUDY AEROBICS

Sharpen Your Skills

Sharpen your essay organization skills by taking your focus off of theme and content. Write a practice essay about a fun topic that you are well-acquainted and comfortable with, such as your favorite television show or movie, your best friend, or your dog. When writing about a topic that means something to you, the words come more easily; this gives you the opportunity to concentrate on the other aspects of essay writing, such as organization, paragraphing, and sentence structure.

TESTING YOUR FRIENDSHIPS

Who better to help you hone your skills than a friend? Like Gene, Nita, and Tomoyuki, you can create a study group in which you provide encouragement and advice to help group members identify their weaknesses, further hone their strengths, and perform to their potential. Some things to remember are:

- **It is study time, not social time.**
  Remember that studying with friends can be much more enjoyable than studying alone, but this is not social time. It is important that all members of your study group remain focused.

- **Be positive!**
  Try to keep your study group sessions serious but upbeat. The purpose of your group is to help and encourage each other, not to spend the time lamenting about how unfair the test is likely to be.

- **Critique, don't criticize.**
  Remember to be positive in your feedback to your friends. Critiquing is a positive process in which advice and tips are given using positive tones and sentences. Also remember that when your work is being critiqued, you should not take offense to a friend pointing out errors or areas where you could improve your work.

MINDBENDER

Play Matching Games

- Print out a bunch of free response questions and writing prompts along with appropriate sample answers and essays. Separate the questions from their answers and try to match them again. This exercise will help you recognize the structural differences between essays and free response answers and will also help you pay attention to the specific details and requirements of each question and prompt.

- Find sample essays, cut them up into separate sentences, and try to piece the essays back together again. When you have finished, compare your version with the original. Is your version organized in a similar fashion or do the ideas seem disorganized?

- Delete every third or fourth word from a few sample essays; then, paying close attention to sentence structure and the requirements of the writing prompt, go back and try to fill in the blanks. When you have finished, compare your version with the original. Do they both convey the same ideas, or did your word choice drastically change the tone of the essay? Did the remaining words offer thematic clues that you may have overlooked?

Just the Facts

- Always read the instructions and the questions carefully.
- Prior to writing your answer, organize your thoughts.
- Identify key words and use those words in your responses.
- Study with friends to gain a pre-test assessment of your work.

Secret 4

MASTERING YOUR
STUDY ENVIRONMENT

Jamie was thrilled about entering high school, but she was unable to raise her grades to the level she and her parents expected.

Jamie studied at the dining room table as she always had, with her back to the living room, tuning out the noises of the television or her parents and younger sister playing games. She tried spending more time studying but found that the extra time didn't make a difference. She wanted to learn the material her teachers assigned, but Jamie also wanted to relax with her family.

Now that studying had become difficult for Jamie, all sorts of things came to mind for her to do during her study time. She visited the kitchen hunting for snacks. She remembered chores she had not completed and notes she needed to write. She even found herself playing with the salt and pepper shakers on the table.

Jamie felt her freshman year slipping away.

Do you understand what Jamie is feeling? She has conflicting goals, studying and relaxing with her family, and she is easily distracted in the setting she has placed herself in. Aha! There is the clue: "she has placed herself in." Jamie is, as all students are, responsible for creating her own study environment, including where, when, and how she studies.

This chapter explains how to master *your* study environment to improve *your* test scores.

ACTIVE STUDY TIME

Essential to improving your test scores is making your study time *active*. Many of us approach studying in a *passive* way—we just absorb facts and theories like a sponge. We may think that because we have read the textbook, heard the lecture, and taken notes, we're all set. This book is about your investment in a more *active* role in your study process. Let's get to it.

Some examples of active studying include:

- researching your tests
- setting your goals
- creating and implementing a study plan
- asking questions
- exploiting resources
- brainstorming additional ideas and connections
- organizing your notes
- mastering your study environment

Consider yourself an active student at the start of each course and each class period. It will take some practice, but you can do it. And how do you implement active studying? Start with the right *attitude*!

THE RIGHT ATTITUDE

Hey, it may seem corny, but it's empowering to have a good attitude. What do you think of these examples of positive attitude?

- *Mae acknowledges that to be a veterinarian when she's an adult, she will have to work hard now, especially around exam times.* Mae accepts a commitment to hard work.

- *Teddy pretends he's a super academic athlete, shifting into active test-training mode when a test is coming up.* Teddy uses an image that will help him enjoy his studies more.

- *Phil gladly helps Tera with her French, and Tera knows how to explain their ecology assignments in ways that Phil can understand.* Phil believes that "what goes around, comes around," so he gets satisfaction from helping others.

- *Candy takes advantage of a variety of learning opportunities: She reads the extra assignment, looks for resources online, watches PBS, and asks questions in class.* Candy is enthusiastic and curious.
- *Noi considers how to apply what she has learned in books and in class to her life.* Noi extends her knowledge to other applications.
- *Drew hates making mistakes but tries to learn from them, make the best of things, and accept that taking risks may involve failure.* Drew can turn lemons into lemonade.

Create an Attitude that Invites Success

Be sure to create the right attitude about study and especially about reading—students do a lot of it! If you have something challenging to read and you tell yourself, "I'll never understand this," chances are that you won't. You have conditioned yourself for failure. Instead, condition yourself for success. Give yourself affirmations such as:

- "No matter how hard the reading level, I will learn something from this."
- "I will become a better reader with each reading task."
- "I can understand and I will remember."

Have a positive attitude about your reading material, too. If you tell yourself, "This is going to be boring," you undermine your chances for learning and enjoying. Even if you are not interested in the topic you have to read about, remember that you are reading it for a reason: You have something to gain. Keep your goals clearly in mind. Remember, it's OK to reward yourself when you have completed a difficult reading assignment. (And the knowledge you gain from the reading is also its own reward.)

What if you have mastered the right attitude, but still can't concentrate on your studies? Maybe you should look into mastering *brain interference*, too!

WHAT EXACTLY IS BRAIN INTERFERENCE?

Can you focus on the task in front of you? Do you know how to eliminate brain interference?

In *Study Smarts*, authors Judi Kesselman-Turkel and Franklynn Peterson suggest that the most effective tip for concentrating is to eliminate "brain interference"—whatever distracts you from your ability to focus. Brain interference can range from being in love to wondering if your sister's birthday is on Monday or Tuesday.

Try these suggestions to free your brain from interference:

- If you are hungry, cold, hot, or sleepy, take care of it.

- If you are a nibbler, have healthy snacks nearby before you start to study.

- If you have nervous habits, such as twirling your hair or biting your nails, ask yourself if they calm you or distract you. If they distract you, think of a non-distracting substitute, such as holding a highlighter in your hand.

- If you need to have music or noise in the background, try Mozart or white noise. Music by Mozart has been proven to adjust brainwaves to their most receptive state; studying while listening to the Sonata for Two Pianos in D Major the night before exams improved students' test scores! For white noise, try turning on a fan to create a consistent background noise that will mask any interrupting noises (TV in another room, your little brother's play group) that could occur as you settle in for a study session.

- If you keep thinking about irrelevant details (deadlines, questions to ask your coach, lyrics to a song), write them down, make lists, and keep a written or electronic calendar so that you can focus on studying instead.

- If you are studying courses with similar concepts, such as physics and calculus, you should separate them on your study schedule to keep vocabulary and formulas clear.

- If you are experiencing emotional interference—you are angry at your teacher or in trouble with your dad—talk it out with a friend, parent, or mentor.

- If you are anxious about passing a chemistry course, your anxiety may actually help motivate you to remember better. However, if you are anxious about a dentist appointment, turn your thinking back to studying.

NURTURE CONCENTRATION

Do you know someone who can concentrate with laser-like attention? Some of us can do this naturally, but most of us need to set the stage for good concentration. Since good concentration leads to more efficient studying, which leads to more effective test taking, consider these steps:

1. **Make yourself a special study spot:** *Roy studies on the side table in his mom's home office.* (Read more on special study spots later in this chapter.)

2. **Choose one goal at a time—a small, specific, and reasonable task:** *Gia is memorizing the first half of the Periodic Table of the Elements.*

3. **Prepare the space for work—gather a dictionary, calculator, and extra paper—and then begin:** *Jason made sure he had 3 sharpened pencils for his practice exam.*

4. **When you finish a task, leave your study spot and take a break:** *Rachel walked to the kitchen for some orange juice and a chat with her dad.*

5. **Gradually increase the amount of work you want to get done in a study session:** *Tomoyuki discovered that, with practice and breaks, he could study for his SATs for an entire afternoon without losing concentration.*

The idea is to reward yourself for *good* concentration. Too many of us work until we can't concentrate any longer and aren't getting much done, and then we take a break. When you think about it, this is merely rewarding *bad* concentration.

SOURCES IN CYBERSPACE

Concentration Sites
Check out this URL for a list of links to sites and articles on how to concentrate when studying. There are some excellent tips to try.

- www.howtostudy.org/resources/conc/index.htm

Article titles include:

- Concentration and Reading
- Concentration and Your Body
- Studying with Intensity
- Concentration and Distraction

DID WE MENTION TO MAKE TIME FOR STUDY BREAKS?

Why not make time for a study break after each hour or after a reasonable task is finished? If you do, you will definitely be able to retain more information, and your body will feel less tension. Again, you are rewarding yourself for *good* concentration—for putting in those 60 minutes of study effort!

For every hour of study, Evan does two reps of his stretching routine. He likes the feeling of renewed energy and of doing something physical between the mental exercises.

Berta takes a short five-minute break after reading a textbook assignment. She finds that when she writes down her summary *after* the break, she remembers more of what she read and how it fits into the big picture.

Hector closes his eyes for ten minutes between studying different subjects. Some basic yoga breathing and meditation make him feel refreshed and help separate the subjects in his mind.

Finally, let's be realistic. Do you ever have trouble resisting the urge to slack off? It might help to remember these words of Victor Frankl, founder of one of the Vienna schools of psychology:

> Live as if you were living already for the second time and as if you had acted the first time as wrongly as you are about to act now! It seems that there is nothing that would stimulate a man's sense of responsibility more than this maxim, which invites him to imagine first that the present is past and, second, that the past may yet be changed and amended. Such a precept confronts him with life's *finiteness* as well as the *finality* of what he makes out of both his life and himself.
>
> —Victor Frankl, "Logotherapy in a Nutshell," *Man's Search for Meaning*

YOUR SPECIAL STUDY SPOT

Have you ever noticed where kids study in your high school? Out on the lawn, in the hallways, draped over a bleacher bench, in a noisy classroom, in the cafeteria line, at the bus stop—maybe even some-times in study hall and the library.

If you feel that these places don't offer you a place to settle down and spread out your notes with a minimum of distractions, find your-self a special study spot. You can even designate one at home and one at school.

At home, the ideal location is one you can call your own—where you can retreat to study and where you can leave your "stuff." Some ideas for a special study spot at home are:

- a corner of the kitchen or den
- a desk or table in your room
- a cleaned-up area in the garage, basement, or attic
- a large walk-in closet that you have converted into a study

Remember, you will want to be in a well-lit area where you are com-fortable and where you can have your books and papers or computer in easy reach. Add plants or a stick of burning incense if they relax you. Put away or turn off every distraction that might take your mind off of the task ahead! Ask your family not to disturb you or bring you the phone when you are in your study spot.

The Ambience of Your Study Spot

Webster's defines *ambience* as "an environment or its distinct atmos-phere." The environment you study in is a crucial element of your academic success. One experiment in study ambience moved a small group of students from a loud, busy room into a quiet study area, where they accomplished in three hours what had previously taken ten hours!

Your study location may vary. Sally studies at the desk in her bed-room, and Lionel sits against an old tree in the park. In addition to location, the elements that comprise the ambience of your study area are:

- noise or silence
- kind of noise (music, whispering, TV, footsteps in a library)
- lighting (where, what kind, how bright)
- your view (a wall, the woods outside the window)

- temperature of the area (too hot, too cold)
- smells in the area (burned toast, strawberry incense)
- ventilation (stuffy, good air flow, drafty)
- visual movement around you (your siblings wrestling, people walking by)
- furniture (comfort and ergonomics of your chair, desk, study nook)
- emotional connections (relaxed feeling, tension)

Your learning style or styles (see Secret #5) may even contribute to your study ambience. For example, some of us who are rhythmic or musical learners can actually review and retain *better* with music or TV in the background (sorry, Mom). Marie-Teresa, who is a bodily-kinesthetic learner, finds that she remembers the conjugations of Spanish verbs if she paces the room while repeating them! Most of us, however, prefer not to have a lot of visual distractions while studying.

Now, consider all of these elements with your personality and experience. What is *your* ideal environment for studying?

STUDY AEROBICS

A Concentration Exercise: Use a Study Totem

Strengthen your ability to concentrate by selecting a physical symbol that will become associated in your mind with studying. This will be your *study totem*. Select one particular article of clothing, such as a scarf or hat, or a little figurine or knickknack. Just before you start to study, put on your red ski cap or set your little study totem on the desk. The ceremony will aid concentration in two ways. First of all, it will be a signal to other people that you are working and that they should not disturb you. Second, going through a short, regular ritual will help you get down to work. Be sure that you don't use your study totem when you are writing letters, daydreaming, or just horsing around. Keep it just for studying. If your charm becomes associated with anything besides books, get a new one. You must be very careful that it doesn't become a symbol for daydreaming.

STUDY TOOLS

"The right tool for the right job" may be an expression your father used to love to repeat (and you would roll your eyes, right?). Well, he was correct. Why waste your time and effort with the improper tool? You wouldn't hammer a nail in the wall with a screwdriver, would you? The same is true of study tools. For example, don't practice for a geometry test with a permanent marker!

In fact, selecting the right study tool is a much overlooked but very important consideration for mastering your study environment. Let's start with furniture and computers.

Furniture and Computer Accessories

You should use a chair and desk or laptop board that are comfortable, but not so comfortable that you will fall asleep. You should look for proper back support and good ventilation in your study furniture. Most people like to write on a flat surface such as a table or desk, but some students prefer the angle of a drafting table.

If you are sitting at a computer, you should have an ergonomically designed chair that is the right height and the best distance from the monitor. You might choose to add a lumbar pad for additional back support. Depending on how long you sit at the computer, you may try a leg rest or foot stool to relieve your lower back and lower legs. You may also want to buy a wrist support for your mouse pad or keyboard. There are keyboards available that are shaped for better reach when typing and less possibility of carpal tunnel syndrome (wrist stress). Some people buy a special screen to cut down on monitor glare and eyestrain.

Study Supplies

Try to study in a cleared space. Prepare your study area with what you may need *before* you sit down, such as:

- textbooks, manuals, lab books
- lecture notes
- flashcards
- practice tests
- blank index cards

- pens and sharpened pencils
- correction fluid
- measuring and calculating tools such as a calculator, ruler, and compass

Resources

Ask yourself, "What resource tools might I need to study for this test?"

- dictionary
- thesaurus
- encyclopedia
- periodicals and books
- software
- list of websites

MINDBENDER

Conduct Your Own Study Environment Analysis

The goal of this analysis is to help you evaluate the three places you study most frequently. Begin by identifying those three locations in the blanks below. List them in the order that you use them, from most frequently to least frequently used. Then answer each question according to whether the statement is mostly true (T) or mostly false (F) about each of the three places you have identified.

Place A = _____

Place B = _____

Place C = _____

	PLACE A	PLACE B	PLACE C
1. There are few distractions, such as a phone, computer, or TV, in this location.			
2. Other people rarely interrupt me when I study in this location.			
3. This is a quiet location, with almost no interruptions from phones ringing, people talking, or music playing.			

	PLACE A	PLACE B	PLACE C
4. I take a limited number of breaks when I study in this environment.			
5. I study here regularly during the week.			
6. I tend to keep my breaks short when I study in this location.			
7. I rarely talk with people when I study here.			
8. The temperature in this place is very comfortable for study-ing most of the time.			
9. The chair in this place is very conducive to studying.			
10. The desk or table in this place is very conducive to studying.			
11. The lighting in this place is very conducive to studying.			
12. There are few things in this location that are unrelated to studying or school work.			

Inventory devised by Virginia Polytechnic Institute, Cook Counseling Center

When you have answered all 12 questions, add the number of "True" responses you gave for each of the three places. The place with the highest total is probably your best environment for studying.

Just the Facts

- Take an *active* role in studying.
- Empower yourself with a positive attitude.
- Eliminate brain interference, such as physical and emotional distractions.
- Nurture concentration by practicing the steps on how to focus.
- Make time for study breaks—reward your concentration, don't undermine it.
- Create a study ambience that will foster comfort and efficiency. Pay attention to noise, lighting, ventilation, movement, and furniture.
- Select the right study tools for the job at hand, including furniture, computer accessories, materials, and resources.

Secret 5

DISCOVERING YOUR LEARNING STYLE

Nikia, Ann, Christy, Linda, and Colleen were more than friends—they had known each other since nursery school. Now, they were high school sophomores. Each wanted to improve her grades, so Nikia, a natural leader, suggested they form a study group.

The study group was a disaster. Linda only wanted to tell stories. Christy, a born artist, gravitated toward pictures, and Ann, who was most comfortable studying on her own, hated all the arguments.

Colleen suggested they conduct an experiment: break the material they were studying into pieces. Each person would study and explain her piece of the material any way she liked. It seemed like a crazy idea, so Linda liked it immediately.

Gradually, the idea worked. The girls mixed their learning styles. Nikia kept the group focused, and Ann watched to make sure everyone had a chance to contribute. The girls mixed their learning styles. Not everything worked, however. Ann grew tired of Linda's crossword puzzles based on the names of Revolutionary War generals. But Christy's diagram of Bunker Hill helped them all visualize the battle. Linda read aloud from the diaries of soldiers. Colleen created a table showing the men, materials, and casualties for each

side, and Nikia finally understood the cost of eighteenth-
century warfare.

   Nikia drew several helpful diagrams, and shy Ann even
led two study group meetings. No one except Linda
wanted to create crossword puzzles based on generals'
names.

Does the girls' study group work? It would seem so. Or maybe only
when Nikia can keep such a gathering of diverse learners in focus! Did
you identify with anyone in the story?

   Which learning styles do *you* use when studying? **Learning
styles** are different approaches to thinking and absorbing material.
We not only learn at different paces, but also in different ways.
Most of us have at least one dominant style, but all students use a
combination of learning styles—depending on the activity they are
involved in.

WHAT KIND OF LEARNER ARE YOU?

You are a unique learner: No one else processes information in
exactly the same way you do. When you discover the ways you learn
best, you can expand the strategies you use for learning and studying. Ultimately, this will mean more efficient learning and test
taking.

   Consider how you learn a new piece of information. For example,
when a friend gives you his or her phone number, how you do learn
and remember it?

Do you see the numbers in your head?

Do you say the numbers, perhaps over and over, in your head?

Do you say the numbers out loud?

Do you write the numbers in the air with your finger?

Do you make a picture of the numbers?

Do you hear the tones of the numbers?

Do you put the numbers in certain groupings?

Think about what you like to do and what comes easily to you. Usually you are comfortable doing certain activities, and you get more out

of these activities because they match your learning style. Do you doodle? Do you love role-playing games? Are you a list maker? Are you always active? These are clues to your learning style.

Let's explore two major approaches to learning: Right-Brain/Left-Brain and Gardner's Multiple Intelligences.

Right-Brain, Left-Brain

One well-known approach to learning deals with whether the right side or the left side of your brain is dominant. Modern scientists know that your left brain is your verbal and rational brain, and your right brain is your nonverbal and intuitive brain. You require special functions from both sides of your brain to accomplish most tasks in your daily life. However, there are some nonverbal tasks—such as drawing, painting, dancing and music, at which your right brain excels and you would be better off shelving your left brain functions to prevent interference from your rational side.

The two sides do communicate with each other, though, and you will recognize aspects of your thinking process in both sides. Although most people can be categorized as left- or right-brain thinkers, there are exercises that can help you develop and nurture either side. You can explore websites on the subject or even take a free brain-dominance test at: brain.web-us.com/brain/LRBrain.html.

Right-Brain Thinkers

Right-brain or *creative thinkers* (such as artists, composers, and poets):

- are usually left-handed
- gather information by feelings and intuition
- do not use a step-by-step process to gather information—rather, it is visually gathered all at once
- retain information by using images and patterns and are able to visualize the whole idea
- may seem illogical or disorganized because they are emotional, intuitive, and abstract in their thinking
- are good at coming up with innovative ideas

Left-Brain Thinkers

Left-brain or *critical thinkers* (such as scientists, accountants, and lawyers):

- are usually right-handed
- are good at organizing
- tend to be more orderly in their thought processes, collecting information using logic and sense
- retain information using words, numbers, and symbols
- see only parts of the whole idea, which guide them in their logical, step-by-step gathering of information
- express themselves with concise words, numerical and written formulas, and high-tech systems

Each kind of thinking has its own strengths. The right-brain thinker will come up with a good theme for a birthday party, but the left-brain thinker is the one you count on to organize the party, send out the invitations, get the food, and find people to help decorate. The right-brain thinker excels at creative games like charades, and the left-brain thinker excels at games that require logic and following rules, like chess. Right-brain thinkers like the rhythm of poetry. Left-brain thinkers like figuring out the meaning of a poem. Are you left- or right-brain dominant?

Tips from Damon for Right-Brain Thinkers

Damon, who studies with Amelia, relates what they study to what he already knows, in very broad ways—often in ways that would not occur to Amelia. Damon is what is called a *global thinker.*

When Damon is trying to understand a text, he uses imagery to visualize the order of events. History class is a challenge for him. "All those dates!" he cries. "They don't make sense to me." Imagining historical events, Damon puts his mental pictures in order, like a cartoon. Sometimes he draws them on paper. He then associated dates with the pictures, using imagery to better understand the order of events.

Damon is good at seeing the big picture, finding themes, and drawing conclusions. He finds speaking his ideas into a tape recorder helpful. Sometimes, Damon uses his imagination to pretend that a textbook section is a speech or a play and he's the announcer or actor. He is often best able to express himself using art, music, or dance.

Tips from Amelia for Left-Brain Thinkers

Amelia is left-brain dominant; she naturally thinks in an orderly way. This is called *sequential thinking*. She notes events and puts them in a sequence to understand them. Amelia's poetry class is a challenge—all those images! So she turns her reading into a kind of detective story, asking herself, "What happened first? Then what happened? What next? What led up to the ending?" It is her sense of sequence that allows her to create outlines of what happens in the poem and translate them to images.

Amelia also rewrites her class notes in list or outline form, putting details under major topic headings. She reads her notes into a tape recorder and plays them back. She breaks her subjects into parts, forming categories and subgroups. Timelines and formulas help her remember data. Amelia takes advantage of her strong skills in deductive, rational, and concrete analysis.

Gardner's Multiple Intelligences

Author Christopher Koch writes,

> When Michael Jordan performs an inexplicable maneuver in the air above a basketball court or Luciano Pavarotti extracts another shimmering high C from the gristle of his vocal chords, we don't necessarily think of either of these men as being intelligent. They might be, but we assume these talents to be peripheral to intelligence rather than proof of it.
>
> Howard Gardner, a Harvard University professor of education and author, disagrees. When Jordan lifts off or Pavarotti opens wide, Gardner sees intelligence—something called bodily kinesthetic intelligence in the case of Jordan and musical intelligence in that of the big tenor. Gardner doesn't limit smarts to the traditional realms of logical reasoning and the ability to manipulate words and numbers. He says we are all endowed with eight distinct forms of intelligence that are genetically determined but can be enhanced through practice and learning.
>
> —Christopher Koch, *CIO Magazine*, March 15, 1996

Dr. Gardner's Multiple Intelligence (MI) Theory recognizes that intelligence can come in many forms:

1. **Verbal/Linguistic Intelligence**—sensitivity to the meaning of words, grammar rules, and the function of language, as in writing

an essay; someone with this kind of intelligence likes to "play with words."

2. **Logical/Mathematical Intelligence**—ability to see relationships between objects and to solve problems, as in calculus and engineering; someone with this kind of intelligence likes to "play with questions."

3. **Visual/Spatial Intelligence**—ability to perceive and mimic objects in different forms or contexts, as in miming or impressionist painting; someone with this kind of intelligence likes to "play with pictures."

4. **Musical/Rhythmic Intelligence**—ability to hear tones, rhythms, musical patterns, pitch, and timbre, as in composing a rap or a symphony; someone with this kind of intelligence likes to "play with music."

5. **Body/Kinesthetic Intelligence**—loving movement, using the body and motor systems in the brain to solve a problem, as in catching a ball; someone with this kind of intelligence likes to "play with moving."

6. **Interpersonal Intelligence**—sensitivity to the actions, moods, and feelings of others, as in teaching, parenting, politicking; someone with this kind of intelligence likes to "play with socializing."

7. **Intrapersonal Intelligence**—ability to understand and define inner feelings, as in poetry and therapy; someone with this kind of intelligence likes to "play alone."

8. **Naturalist Intelligence**—sensitivity to animals, plants, and the environment, noticing patterns in nature and caring deeply about nature, as in collecting rocks and minerals; someone with this kind of intelligence likes to "play in nature."

STUDY AEROBICS

Integrating Technology into Multiple Intelligences
Yes, your learning style can be enhanced with technology.

Verbal/Linguistic

- e-mail and chat rooms
- CD-ROMs and software teaching language, writing, editing, and rewriting skills
- desktop publishing programs and multimedia authoring
- programs that allow you to create stories, poems, and essays
- using tape recorders
- browsing the Internet

Logical/Mathematical

- computer programs and games that teach logic and critical thinking skills
- database and spreadsheet programs to organize data
- problem-solving and math software or websites
- Computer Aided Design (CAD) programs
- strategy game software
- graphing calculators

Visual/Spatial

- draw, paint, and 3-D programs
- surfing the Internet
- organizing files and folders to develop spatial understanding
- webpage design
- software games
- spreadsheet programs that allow you to see charts, maps, or diagrams
- multimedia authoring programs

Music/Rhythmic

- music composing software
- CD, CD-ROM, and DVD players
- programs integrating stories with songs and instruments
- CD-ROMs about music and instruments
- tape recorders
- word processors (to write reviews or lyrics)

Body/Kinesthetic

- computer use resulting in better hand-eye coordination
- software games that need keyboard, mouse, joystick, and microphone
- programs that allow you to move objects around the screen
- typing on a typewriter or word processor
- animation programs

Interpersonal

- group work or tutoring with two to four people on computers
- computer games for two or more
- programs for group presentations
- telecommunication programs
- e-mail and chat rooms
- interactive distance learning

Intrapersonal

- any programs in which you work independently and at your own pace
- games for one person
- brainstorming or problem-solving software and websites
- word processors for keeping a journal
- a multimedia portfolio
- video editing

Naturalist

- tape recorder to record nature
- digital or SLR cameras and video cameras to record nature
- software, games, CD-ROMs, and websites on nature topics
- slide or Microsoft PowerPoint projector
- binoculars, telescopes, microscopes, or magnifiers

A Mix of Learning Styles

Some students have one dominant intelligence or learning style, but most of us have a mix of several. For example, Jake, Katie, and Meghan all learn best when they are moving in some way—the ways vary, but they are all kinesthetic learners. Notice their secondary learning styles.

- Jake hates sports, but he's active in other ways. His hands move like butterflies when he speaks, and he hops around a lot! He likes working with people and telling stories and jokes. (Gardner MIs #5, #6, and #1)
- Katie's friends say she's quiet and introspective. She loves knitting. She often doodles when she's studying—in class or on the bus. She feels that knitting and doodling help her think clearly. (Gardner MIs #7, #3, and #5)
- Meghan is a real jock who loves basketball and ice-skating. She dances to any kind of music and hums a lot. In class, she's usually tapping her foot. Meghan is also an avid list maker. (Gardner MIs #5, #4, and #2)

SOURCES IN CYBERSPACE

Learning Styles

- www.dacc.cc.il.us/~kjenkins/selfimprovement.html—**What Is Your Learning Style?** Learning style surveys can be found here.
- www.cio.com/archive/031596_qa.html and www.nea.org/neatoday/9903/gardner.html—**Howard Gardner.** Read two fascinating interviews with the man who developed Multiple Intelligences at these sites.
- www.casacanada.com/book.html—**Bookshelf of Multiple Intelligences.**

THE NINE INTELLIGENCES

1. Verbal/Linguistic Intelligence: Using Language Effectively

Does this sound like you? Do you:

- have a rich vocabulary and a sensitivity to the meanings of words?
- like to tell, write, and listen to stories?

- enjoy listening and talking to people?
- like word games, word play, jokes, and puzzles?
- sort information through your listening and repeating skills?

Your Study Style

You probably love to read, write, and listen to the beauty and richness of language; you may be interested in word derivations, grammar, and definitions. You like word play, puns, jokes, and word games such as crosswords. You may be the class clown or the most sympathetic listener. You are most likely an excellent note taker. You benefit from studying with a partner and taking turns reading, speaking, and listening about your subjects together.

Tips

- Play reporter, interviewing people for a report or a family history.
- Listen to books-on-tape in the car or on a Walkman.
- Write poetry, short stories, articles, and plays.
- Tape lectures and listen to them when rewriting notes.
- Repeat vocabulary or conjugations out loud in the shower or while walking.
- Write new lyrics to a familiar tune.

2. Logical/Mathematical Intelligence: Using Numbers Effectively

Does this sound like you? Do you:

- have a strong curiosity about how things work?
- like to ask questions and investigate?
- use numbers wisely and enjoy solving problems?
- have the ability to understand logical patterns, categories and relationships, and causes and effects?
- enjoy strategy games, logic puzzles, and experiments?
- like to use computers?

Your Study Style

You have a structured, organized way of thinking. You are good at making lists and charts (sequential thinking). You don't always want to know exactly what something is because you prefer to figure it out yourself. You probably like algebra better than arithmetic. The meanings in short stories, novels, or poems come easily to you.

Tips

- Make outlines to help align your thinking, as you review old material and add new information.
- Practice exercises called *syllogisms*, such as "If A = B, and B = C, then A = C."
- Solve logic puzzles, games, jigsaw puzzles, and riddles.
- Read mysteries or crime investigations and try to figure out the answer.
- Enjoy how-things-work and cross-section books.
- Devise question-and-answer sessions with your study buddy or for your study group.
- Enjoy the Internet and multiple software programs.

3. Visual/Spatial Intelligence: Thinking in Images

Does this sound like you? Do you:

- easily visualize three-dimensional objects?
- take information and translate it into images and pictures in your mind?
- retrieve information through images and pictures you have stored earlier?
- enjoy geometry and recognize the relationships of objects in space?
- like to look at or create drawings, sculptures, or crafts?
- get called a "daydreamer"?

Your Study Style

You are probably successful in geometry and very good in visual arts, sculpture, architecture, and photography. You may enjoy mazes and jigsaw puzzles and spend your free time drawing or building. You probably like to see the "whole picture" (global thinking) and often don't need to work through individual parts, as sequential learners do.

Tips

- Turn what you're reading into your own cartoon or storyboard.
- Pay attention to the "movie" in your head. Draw pictures that come to mind in the margins of your texts, or in your notes.
- Write or record a summary using doodles, symbols, and colors.
- Film a report or design a newsletter with desktop software.
- Write stories and reports from photographs or paintings, or from video or educational TV.

4. Musical/Rhythmic Intelligence: Understanding and Expressing Music and Rhythm

Does this sound like you? Do you:

- have the ability to hear and recognize tones, rhythms, and musical patterns?
- show sensitivity to nonverbal sounds in the environment?
- play an instrument or belong to a choir?
- remember and repeat a melody after listening to it once?
- enjoy listening to music and singing to yourself?

Your Study Style

You have a wonderful ability to understand the structure of music, to create melodies and rhythms. You can learn through rhythm and melody. You prefer to have music in the background when studying, and you learn new things more easily if sung, tapped, or whistled. You are probably an *auditory learner*, preferring to *hear* a lecture or a tape.

- Listen to books-on-tape and lectures in the car and on your Walkman.
- Turn information into a rap or song lyrics.
- Study with Mozart playing in the background; his music has been proven to align the brain's rhythms.
- Dance or move around to music while reciting.
- Tap your foot or fingers as you read your text as if it were a song or poem. This works with math and science formulas, too.

5. Body/Kinesthetic Intelligence: Using the Body and Movement to Express Oneself

Does this sound like you? Do you:

- need to touch and manipulate things?
- tend to move, jump, hop around, and fidget?
- learn better when doing hands-on work, such as a science experiment or building a model?
- like participating in or watching games, sports, acrobatics, or acting?

Your Study Style

You are more successful in learning if you can touch, manipulate, and move or feel whatever you are learning. You do well with physical activities: games, acting, hands-on tasks, and building. You probably process information through movement or watching movement, like when historical scenes are acted out or when given an assignment to build a bridge out of toothpicks.

Tips

- During a lecture, doodle or silently tap you finger when you are not writing.
- Rewrite your notes—a physical activity.

- Enjoy crafts, building, and working on mechanical projects.
- Study by moving. After a study session, take a notepad and pen and go for a 20-minute walk. Stop and write down thoughts on what you studied as they come to mind.
- Use a computer—this involves constant action, and there is a lot of action on the screen, too.
- Learn by watching TV or videos, such as the History, Discovery, and Travel Channels.

6. Interpersonal Intelligence: Understanding People and Relationships

Does this sound like you? Do you:

- understand and care about other people's feelings?
- notice facial expressions, gestures, and voices?
- recognize differences among people and value their points of view with sensitivity to their motives, moods, and intentions?
- have a lot of friends?
- maintain good relationships with family and friends?

Your Study Style

You are good at working with a partner or in study groups. You listen well and contribute, too, interacting effectively with those around you—teachers and fellow students. You like to teach other kids and take part in school organizations and clubs. You have the ability to influence people, and you are probably a natural leader.

Tips

- Study and review with others, bouncing ideas off of them.
- When working with a study buddy, you can each become a different character and discuss—or debate—the topic you are studying.
- Use your empathetic skills to try to understand the motivations and decisions of political science, history, and science leaders.

- Brainstorm and problem-solve with friends, do practice tests, and discuss class notes together.

7. Intrapersonal Intelligence: Understanding Oneself

Does this sound like you? Do you:

- have an awareness of your own strengths, weaknesses, feelings, and moods?
- prefer to study and play alone?
- use your self-knowledge and self-discipline to reach your goals?
- monitor your thoughts and feelings and control them pretty well?
- learn best through observing and listening?

Your Study Style

You are self-motivated and prefer to study on your own without distractions. You are also analytical and prone to introspection. You enjoy solitary activities like reading and writing. You process information internally, challenging your own thoughts and assumptions with ease. You may be quiet or shy in class and have trouble speaking up in a group setting.

Tips

- Use your self-knowledge to set up the best study plan for your goals.
- Design a quiet, private space for studying and ask for cooperation from your family.
- Role play: If you are studying management, pretend you own your own company; if you're studying chemistry, think of yourself as a chemist.
- Try reading and writing while walking around the house.
- Act out what you have learned. Nobody's watching—your character can even be a machine if that's what you are learning about.
- Talk to yourself as you review materials from a tape, notes, or a reading.

8. Naturalist Intelligence: Connecting with Nature

Does this sound like you? Do you:

- care about plants, animals, the environment, and endangered species?
- like to collect rocks, flowers, or seeds?
- show strong interest in natural sciences such as biology, astronomy, meteorology, and zoology?
- examine and notice patterns and characteristics in nature?
- enjoy outdoor activities, such as hiking and camping?
- like to read or watch shows about animals and plants and the environment?

Your Study Style

You have a strong connection to the outside world and enjoy outdoor activities. You notice patterns and things from nature easily and may have nature collections. You probably enjoy text, stories, and shows that deal with natural events. You learn characteristics, names, and other nature-related data easily.

Tips

- Research and create an outreach project on the environment or an endangered species.
- Read and study for tests while walking or sitting outside.
- Volunteer at you local animal shelter, or train a Seeing Eye or hearing dog.
- Collect and identify the types of flowers, bugs, and trees in your neighborhood.
- Lead your class or study group on a nature hike.
- Practice biking, camping, fishing, or gardening, and keep a journal of your progress.
- Watch *National Geographic*, the Discovery Channel, or other programming that explores wildlife.

9. Existential Intelligence

Dr. Gardner has recently suggested a ninth intelligence to include people who enjoy thinking and questioning and are curious about deep unknowns such as life and death, space, time, and truth. This category would include thinkers like Aristotle, Plato, Confucius, Ralph Waldo Emerson, Albert Einstein, and Margaret Mead.

Students with this intelligence might pose and ponder questions such as "Why are we here on Earth?", "Is there life on other planets?", "Where do living things go after they die?", and "Who were the famous philosophers and what did they conclude?"

MINDBENDER

Activity Chart for Multiple Intelligences

Verbal/Linguistic	Use storytelling to explain a process. Arrange a debate. Write a poem, myth, legend, short play, or news article. Create a talk show radio program. Conduct an interview.
Logical/Mathematical	Translate material into a mathematical formula or a timeline. Design and conduct an experiment. Make up syllogisms and analogies. Describe the patterns or symmetry in a subject.
Visual/Spatial	Chart, map, cluster, or graph. Create a slide show, videotape, or photo album. Create a piece of art that demonstrates a theory. Invent a board or card game. Illustrate, draw, paint, sketch, or sculpt.
Musical/Rhythmic	Give a presentation with appropriate musical accompaniment. Sing a rap or song that explains the material. Explain how the music of a song is similar to a literary theme. Make an instrument and use it to demonstrate the material.

Body/Kinesthetic	Create a movement or sequence of movements to explain the material. Make task or puzzle cards. Build or construct a model. Plan and attend a field trip. Bring hands-on aids to demonstrate the material.
Interpersonal	Conduct a meeting to address an issue. Participate in a service project. Teach or tutor. Practice giving and receiving feedback.
Intrapersonal	Set and pursue learning goals. Describe one of your personal values. Keep a journal. Assess your own work on a project.
Naturalist	Create observation notebooks of nature. Describe changes in the local or global environment. Care for pets, wildlife, gardens, or parks. Use binoculars, telescopes, microscopes, or magnifiers. Draw or photograph natural objects.

Adapted from Casa Canada at www.casacanada.com/mulin.html

Just the Facts

- Discover your learning styles by thinking about how you acquire and retain new information.

- One philosophy of learning styles is the right-brain (creative)/left-brain (critical) approach.

- Dr. Howard Gardner devised Multiple Intelligences (MI), characteristics that are inherited but can also be influenced by environment.

- The MIs are Verbal/Linguistic, Logical/Mathematical, Visual/Spatial, Musical/Rhythmic, Body/Kinesthetic, Interpersonal, Intrapersonal, Naturalist, and Existential.

- You may have one dominant intelligence or a mixture.

Secret 6

CREATING AND IMPLEMENTING A STUDY PLAN

Janine had only three months left to study for the SAT exam, and she was beginning to get anxious. There was so much information to learn and review. How could she possibly get it all done? Every time she thought about the exam, she felt sick to her stomach.

During lunch, she mentioned her anxiety about the test to her friend Nicole. "Even if I went without sleep and meals for the next two months, I still couldn't get it all done," she sighed.

"Oh, you'll be fine," said Nicole as she opened a can of soda.

"Do you have any idea how many geometry formulas there are? You have to know how to find the area and volume of every shape known to man. And then there's the algebra. Quadratic equations, polynomials—"

"Poly-what?" asked Nicole.

"Polynomials," Janine repeated. "And that's just the math. Don't even get me started on the verbal."

Nicole frowned. "It *does* sound like a lot."

"That's because it *is* a lot," Janine explained. "This is probably one of the most important tests we'll ever take. Have you started studying yet?" Nicole shook her head. "Aren't you nervous?" Janine asked.

"*Now,* I am," Nicole sighed.

Like Janine and Nicole, we sometimes put off structured studying because the task seems too big to handle. The idea of the SAT exam or the ACT assessment can be overwhelming. However, you can make any study schedule for a high stakes test manageable by creating a study plan.

WHAT IS A STUDY PLAN?

Basically, a study plan is an agreement that you make with yourself about how much time and energy you are going to devote to studying for a major exam. This agreement is then broken down into manageable pieces to be tackled before test time.

Follow these four steps to creating a successful study plan for each of your BIG exams coming up this year:

1. **Get the correct information.** Your first step is to find out as much as you can about the exam. Get all the details about the exam, including:
   - When will it be held?
   - Where will it be held?
   - How do you register?
   - When do you need to register?
   - How much does it cost?
   - What do you need to bring with you to the exam?
   - What exactly will be tested on the exam? (What subjects? What kinds of questions?)

2. **Find out what you already know and what you need to learn.** To create an effective study plan, you need to have a good sense of exactly what you need to study. Chances are you already know some of the test material well. Some of it you may only need to review, and some of it you may need to study in detail. If possible, take a practice exam to find out how you would do on the actual exam. How did you score? What do you seem to know well? What do you need to review? What do you need to study in detail?

3. **Set a time frame.** Once you have a good sense of how much studying is ahead, create a detailed study schedule. Use a calendar to set specific deadlines. If deadlines make you nervous, give

yourself plenty of time for each task; otherwise, you might have trouble staying calm and keeping on track.

4. **Break your studying into small chunks that will lead you to your goal step by step**. A study plan that says "Learn everything by May 1" isn't going to be helpful. However, a study plan that sets dates for learning specific material in March and April *will* enable you to learn everything by May 1. For example, if you have 3 months to focus on building your critical reading skills for the SAT or ACT exam, you might create a schedule like the following:

Week 1	Review basic reading comprehension strategies. Start vocabulary list.
Week 2	Practice finding main idea and specific detail questions.
Week 3	Practice vocabulary in context questions.
Week 4	Practice inference questions and finding references in text.
Week 5	Take reading comprehension practice test.
Week 6	Begin reviewing grammar and usage rules. Start reading novel.
Week 7	Review vocabulary.
Week 8	Practice critical reading questions.
Week 9	Practice critical reading questions. Review vocabulary.
Week 10	Take practice test. Finish novel.
Week 11	Start overall review.
Week 12	Continue overall review and taper all week to test day on Saturday.

As you set your deadlines, think carefully about your day-to-day schedule. How much time can you spend on studying each week? Exactly when can you fit in the time to study? Be sure to be realistic about how much time you have and how much you can accomplish. Give yourself the study time you need to succeed.

5. **Stick to your plan.** Make sure you have your plan written on paper and posted on the bulletin board in your room, on the refrigerator, or even in your locker. (Don't just keep it in your head!) Look at it regularly so that you can remember what and when to study. Checking your plan regularly will also help you see how much progress you have made along the way.

It's very important that you *don't give up* if you fall behind. Unexpected events may interrupt your plans. You may have to put in extra time on the yearbook committee; you may have to deal with a problem at home, or you may even come down with the flu. Or it might just take you longer to get through a task than you planned. That's okay. Stick to your schedule as much as possible, but remember that sometimes life gets in the way.

For example, if you have a family problem that's keeping you from concentrating, you may need to postpone your studies to take care of that problem. Just remember to reschedule your study time. Better to study later when you can concentrate than to waste time "studying" when you are unable to focus.

So, if you miss one of your deadlines, don't despair; just pick up where you left off. Try to squeeze in a little extra time during the next few weeks to catch up. If that doesn't seem possible, simply adjust your schedule. Change your deadlines so that they are more realistic. Just be sure you still have enough time to finish everything before the exam.

Consider your study plan as a contract holding you to certain rules for studying. Essentially, your study plan will put you on the fast track for exam success, as well as provide you with answers to the whos, whats, whens, and wheres of your study activities—the topics of the rest of this chapter. As you may have guessed, the creation and implementation of a study plan fits hand in hand with successful time management. For that reason, you will benefit the most by referring to Secret #1 after reading this chapter.

Note: Study plans are different than study schedules. Your study schedule is for everyday school stuff; your study plan is for the BIG EXAM!

SOURCES IN CYBERSPACE

Creating a Study Plan

- www.columbia.edu/cu/augustine/study/schedule.html—Tips for creating and implementing a study plan.
- www.clt.cornell.edu/campus/learn/LSC%20Resources/ Studyguidelines.pdf—Guidelines for creating a study schedule from Cornell University.

Because there are many variables included in study plans, and because each test taker has unique needs and different time frames in which to study, no two study plans will be the same. Bear in mind that the plan you create for the SAT exam is going to differ from the plan you create for your state exit exams. Every time you begin to think about a high stakes test, think first about starting a fresh study plan. As you get ready to create your study plan, ask yourself these important questions.

Who

Who does this study plan affect? Will you be studying independently, with a study group or partner, or with a tutor?

Obviously, your study plan will include you, but are there others who will be affected by the plan? You may be involved in a study group or evening class that meets two times a week or on Saturday mornings. Be sure to include this in your study plan. If you have a parent or tutor assisting you as you prepare for a major test, note those sessions in your study plan as well. Remember, anyone whose help you depend on to help you with test preparation should be mentioned in your plan. On a related note, do not arbitrarily include friends on your study plan just because you think that you *might* study with them sometimes. Only include those people with whom you know you will be studying for your high stakes exam.

What

What are you going to be studying? How will you prioritize your work? Create a list of all of the subject areas on the test that will require your attention. The SAT exam has math and verbal sections; the ACT exam has English, reading, science, and math sections; Advanced Placement tests cover only one subject per exam, but you may have two AP exams in one month, so you may wish to combine them, for example, in an English–Calculus study plan.

Make some general decisions about which segments of the exam require the largest portion of your study energy, and be sure that you leave plenty of time for them in your schedule. For example, if you are a math whiz, you may need to spend more time on your vocabulary lists when studying for the SAT exam.

You may be faced with the dilemma of what to schedule and when. How you prioritize your study time is as important as deciding which topics to study. You know best when you are at your intellectual peak and are most able to grasp and retain facts. You also know which subjects are not as mentally taxing for you. Depending on your learning style, you may want to review your most difficult topics first or only on certain days of the week. For example, you may decide that AP U.S. history requires a half hour of your time every day, but you may schedule just a small block of time once a week for chemistry formulas for your ACT exam. Refer back to Secret #5 for more on learning styles.

When

How much time are you going to allot to studying for the Big Exam, and where are you going to find that time? Use a planner to chart where your time commitments and obligations fall throughout the week. Using this chart, look for study opportunities. There are often short, unacknowledged windows of time in which to study. Using the fifteen minutes when you first arrive at school in the morning to review your Spanish vocabulary for your exit exam provides you with an extra hour and fifteen minutes per week of study time. Likewise, time spent checking your trig formulas on the bus or reviewing your notes on *Lord of the Flies* prior to the homeroom bell really add up!

Be sure that you are honest with yourself when making decisions about your time. Obviously, you will not benefit if you prefer to socialize during those fifteen minutes rather than study. If you are honest with yourself about that fact, you won't make the mistake of tricking yourself into thinking that you will use that time for academics when, in reality, you won't.

Where

Part of your study plan includes where you will study. Will you be studying at the library, at a friend's house, or in a quiet corner of your bedroom? Although some students are able to study effectively at school and during study halls, others prefer to study away from the school atmosphere. See Secret #4 for complete information on your study environment.

WHY SHOULD YOU HAVE A STUDY PLAN?

One of the benefits of a study plan is that it provides a self-monitoring technique that will give you a sense of ownership over your work. By creating, implementing, and then sticking to a study plan, you will learn the skills of self-evaluation, reflection, and following a routine as you work toward your goal. Also, by having a study plan, you are able to measure how much time you are devoting to the necessary subject areas. As you take practice tests, you can see how your focused study is paying off. If you are not improving in one or more areas, you can adjust your plan to refocus on those areas you need to work harder on.

HOW TO START A STUDY PLAN

Creating a personal study plan is not difficult. It simply requires that you sit down and make some decisions about what your academic goals are, and how you can best achieve them. It is a good idea to involve an adult or mentor in the creation of your study plan. This person can act as the witness to the contract that you are creating with yourself and can help get you back on your feet if you begin to falter.

MINDBENDER

Simple Questionnaire
A basic study plan can be enhanced by answering these questions.

1. When I study or do homework I need

   a. quiet.   b. soft music.

2. When I study I like to be

   a. alone.   b. near family.

3. I like to study and do homework

   a. as soon as I get home.   b. after I unwind for awhile.

4. The place I will study for the BIG EXAM is _____ .

5. The time I will study for the BIG EXAM is _____ .

6. If I need help with the BIG EXAM I will _____ .

Look at your answers above, show them to your parents, and enhance your plan together.

HOW TO STICK TO YOUR STUDY PLAN

Sticking to your study plan may not always be easy, and it will require a commitment. Your success is going to be directly related to the level of commitment you are willing to give. Share your study plan with others. Let your parents, older siblings, or a trusted teacher in on the contract, so that they can help get you back on track if you begin to slip. Again, posting your basic study plan in a place where you can see it every day will help remind you of the commitment you have made to yourself.

Some tips that may help to keep your study plan on track include the following:

- **Always refer to your study plan and attempt to stay on schedule.**
  Stick as close to your plan as possible. If you find that you are consistently spending more time on a task or subject than you expected, perhaps you need to reassess your plan. Remember, adjusting your plan is fine: It is a guideline; it is not written in stone.

- **Practice, practice, practice.**
  Do not try to reinvent the wheel when studying; use old practice tests and class work assignments. Rework past assignment problems and tackle sample problems from the test sponsor. Visit testing websites and practice skills online.

- **Keep a list of key topics and major concepts.**
  While in class and studying, write down the important items that you need to learn for your exam.

- **Selectively review your texts.**
  When studying, do not completely reread your textbooks and assigned reading. Skim them, use the notes that you have taken in class, and refer to your lists and index cards containing key topics. This will keep your studying free of mental clutter, allowing you to focus on the important concepts that will most likely be found on high stakes exams.

STUDY AEROBICS

Avoid procrastination by creating a study incentive plan. Every time you stick to your weekly study schedule, reward yourself with a favorite activity or meal.

Helpful Reminders:

- **Post-It Notes** come in an assortment of colors and sizes, which makes them perfect for writing out short To Do lists and notes. Stick them on your computer monitor, TV screen, bedroom door, or in other easily visible places to remind yourself of daily tasks.

- **Palm Pilots** (electronic pocket organizers) work like mini-computers and help keep you organized and on schedule no matter where you are.

- **Day planners** also keep you organized and don't require batteries. Keep one in your backpack and remember to write down important dates and assignments throughout the day.

- If you are extremely forgetful, leave yourself an **answering machine or voicemail message** as a backup reminder.

MAKING ADJUSTMENTS

Reassess your progress on a regular basis. You will undoubtedly find that your study plan needs a few adjustments here and there. Ask yourself if you reached your goals. If not, where did you fall short and why? Try to assess your plan every week as you move toward test day. The more you assess your plan, the better you will be able to hone it to your actual needs. Here is Janine's SAT exam study plan.

	SAT STUDY PLAN	JANINE SALAZAR	
	VERBAL	**MATH**	**Saturday Class**
February 1	Take practice exam. Target weakness: critical reading	Take practice exam. Target weakness: algebra	None
Week 1: Feb. 2– Feb. 8	Review reading comprehension strategies. Start running vocabulary list for sentence completions and analogies.	Review quantitative comparison strategies. Practice quadratic equations and formulas. Review geometry theorems from last year. Algebra tutor Thursday 4–5 P.M.	None

	SAT STUDY PLAN	JANINE SALAZAR	
	VERBAL	**MATH**	**Saturday Class**
Week 2: Feb. 9– Feb. 15	Practice main idea and specific detail questions. Create analogy questions from vocab list. Review vocab with Jessica.	Practice word problems. Review fractions. Create flashcards for geometry formulas. Algebra tutor Thursday 4–5 P.M.	None
Week 3: Feb. 16– Feb. 22	Practice vocabulary in context questions. Create sentence completions. Create flashcards for Latin roots.	Review square roots. Review exponents. Review geometry flashcards. Algebra tutor Thursday 4–5 P.M.	None
Week 4: Feb. 23– March 1	Practice inference and reference questions. Review Latin roots flashcards. Practice process of elimination with Jessica.	Practice quantitative comparison questions. Review factors and multiples. Review probability. Algebra tutor Thursday 4–5 P.M.	None
Week 5: March 2– March 8	Take practice test. Re-evaluate strengths and weaknesses. Review vocab flashcards.	Practice geometry questions. Review order of operations. Create flashcards for math laws. Algebra tutor Thursday 4–5 P.M.	Start Saturday program.
Week 6: March 9– March 15	Practice critical reading questions. Create practice analogy questions with Jessica. Spring Break	Take practice test. Reassess plan. No tutor—Spring Break	9:30–11:30 A.M.
Week 7: March 16– March 22	Create flashcards for common prefixes and suffixes. Review parts of speech (for analogy questions). Create more vocab flashcards.	Review math laws flashcards. Review perfect squares. Practice geometry problems.	9:30–11:30 A.M.

	SAT STUDY PLAN	JANINE SALAZAR	
	VERBAL	**MATH**	**Saturday Class**
Week 8: March 23– March 29	Review flashcards for prefixes and suffixes. Review vocab flash-cards. Practice sentence completion with Jessica.	Review absolute value. Review decimals and percentages. Review mean, median, and mode.	9:30–11:30 A.M.
Week 9: March 30– April 5	Review common types of analogies. Review antonyms. Practice critical reading questions.	Practice graph and tables problems. Review polynomials. Practice system of equations problems.	9:30–11:30 A.M.
Week 10: April 6– April 12	Review Latin root flashcards Review all vocab flash-cards. Evaluate study progress with Jessica.	Review coordinate geometry. Practice word problems. Review ratio and rate problems. Algebra tutor Thursday 4–5 P.M.	9:30–11:30 A.M.
Week 11: April 13– April 19	Start overall review.	Start overall review. Algebra tutor Thursday 4–5 P.M.	None
Week 12: April 20– April 26	Continue overall review and taper all week until test day on Saturday.	Continue overall review and taper all week until test day on Saturday. No tutor.	Exam Day!

Just the Facts

- A personal study plan is a contract you make with yourself to help you succeed on each high stakes test.
- You make the important decisions about who, what, when, and where as they apply to your study plan.
- Include an adult, teacher, or mentor in your study plan to help provide support.
- Refer to Secret #1 for tips on managing your time.

Secret 7

GETTING THE MOST OUT OF CLASS

Eleni knew she was shy, but she felt it was simply something she would have to live with.

The problem was that her shyness was interfering with her favorite class—geometry. Eleni envied her classmates who could throw up their hands during class or hang around after class to ask Ms. Hartick a question. The tricks Eleni relied on for her other classes were not working. She couldn't ask for help from a friend because she had no friends taking geometry. She couldn't find answers to some questions by studying her textbook because she didn't understand some of the textbook's explanations. When Ms. Hartick was discussing a new concept or reviewing a difficult problem, Eleni needed an explanation on the spot.

Eleni explained her problem to her boyfriend and was surprised by his response. "I bet other people have the same question you do," Alberto said. "You'd be doing them a favor by asking your question."

The next day, Eleni gathered her courage and raised her hand. Ms. Hartick seemed pleased, and her answer prepared Eleni for the rest of that day's material.

When class was over, Ms. Hartick approached Eleni and said, "Welcome to class."

Some students work extra hard to get the most they can out of their classes. Eleni went as far as to work against her own nature—being shy—to understand geometry better. Two unforeseen benefits of Eleni's question asking are:

- helping other students who had the same questions
- having a closer relationship with Ms. Hartick

Do you hesitate to ask questions because you are shy or because you think you will appear stupid? Do you know how to listen to a lecture? Stay tuned, because this chapter offers multiple techniques for listening and questioning, as well as for working with study groups and study pals.

LISTENING TO A LECTURE

What is a *lecture?* A lecture is a talk given by one person. Lectures have been used in the classroom since medieval times, when books were scarce. At that time, a lecture (French for *reading*) was usually an instructor reading from the only book available, which was handwritten because the printing press had yet to be invented. Today, lectures are sometimes read from books or notes, but often the teacher simply speaks about a subject, perhaps referring to a book or notes occasionally.

Your job as a student in a lecture situation is to be an *active* listener. You want to become involved with what you are hearing. This takes four steps:

1. **absorbing** information

2. **analyzing** what is important to remember or to study later

3. **organizing** ideas

4. **writing** down or drawing the information for future study

Steps 2, 3, and 4 may come in a different order, depending on your listening and learning styles (See Secret #5).

Listening Styles

If you learn best by hearing, you might find that taking notes while you listen distracts you from what you are hearing. To test this, listen to a talk show *without* taking notes; then, on another day, listen to a talk show *while* taking notes. Decide which works better for you. Either way, writing down questions that come to mind—or even key words that will help you recall information—might be helpful.

If you learn best with images, you need to "see" what you are listening to. Doodle or draw pictures, maps, or timelines of what the lecturer is talking about. Use different colored markers to highlight your notes.

If you learn best by using order, you will want to feel a clear order of events while you listen. Make lists and timelines of what the lecturer is saying. Outline the lecture or number points in the margins.

If you learn best by doing and moving, you need the sense that you are experiencing what is being talked about. Try different ways of doing this. For *doing*, you could pretend you are a reporter for a magazine on the subject of the lecture, and you need to take careful notes so your readers will have an accurate understanding of the subject. For *moving*, you might find that you stay focused best by writing down every word or by gently tapping your foot to the rhythm of the lecturer's speech. (Just don't disturb others around you!)

Translating What You Hear into Useful Notes

Depending on the teaching skills of your instructor, you may need to work harder at understanding what he or she has to say and translating his or her words into useful notes. Here are three strategies that instructors use to organize their lectures. Use the same strategies to help you organize your notes:

- beginning—middle—end
- past—present—future
- theme—sub-theme

Some instructors put a lot of stories, jokes, or irrelevant material into their lectures. Do not include this extraneous material in your notes, *unless it helps you to remember a point*. For example: "Organic compounds always contain carbon (pasta carbonara story)." Discover more about memory tricks in Secret #9.

Asking for Help

What if you listen and take notes but still have questions? Whom can you ask for help?

- your teacher (during class, after class, or during tutoring hours)
- your lab partner or study buddy (more on this later in the chapter)
- a member of the class who seems to "get it"
- the class aide or student teacher
- your study group (more on this later in the chapter)

If you don't understand a concept, get help as soon as you can. It is best not to wait until the last minute to get help—your teacher may not be available to you. This is especially important in science or math, where each new lesson is often built upon the previous one.

If you need to meet with a teacher or an aide for extra help, try to prepare specific questions first. You are more likely to get clear, specific answers.

To help her through her Spanish class, Laurie's mom hired a tutor, who is a Spanish major at a nearby college. Laurie had heard two interesting facts about tutors:

1. Hiring a competent tutor for 25% of the course content is as good as hiring one for 100% of the course. Why do you think this is?

   Answer: If you worked with a competent tutor for the *first* 25% of the course, he or she could help you understand the basic, underlying concepts of the subject, for example, how to write proofs for Algebra II. Also, any good tutor would help you organize and prioritize the subject you are studying—skills you could apply to the remaining 75% of the course.

2. A good tutor's grades go up along with the grades of the person being tutored. Why do you think this is?

   Answer: Teaching something to someone else is one of the surest ways to judge what you know and don't know, what you remember and don't remember, and if you know how to paraphrase (restate in your own words) what you have learned. This is why peer tutoring programs are so successful.

STUDY BUDDIES

In any class, it is valuable to get the phone numbers of at least two of your classmates. That way, if you get sick or miss class, you will have fellow students to call to find out what you missed. They may let you copy their notes or their audiotapes of a lecture. If you want to study together or check information—even if it's over the phone—you will have potential study buddies.

At one time or another, everyone has dreaded the idea of studying for a particular exam because the topic was extremely difficult or painfully boring. In such instances, studying with a partner might be the best approach. Studying with someone else is often easier and more enjoyable. The partner, or study buddy, can be a classmate, friend, coworker, or family member.

If your study buddy is studying the same topic you are, you can work as a team in developing questions and finding the answers. If your buddy is someone from outside class or work, she can act as your student as you teach her what you have been studying. She can also act as your coach by asking you such questions as, "What part of this interested you most? Why? What sticks out in your mind?"

SOURCES IN CYBERSPACE

Study Groups
These sites provide tips on *forming* and *running* your study group:

- www4.rmwc.edu/tutor/form_a_study_group.htm
- homeworktips.about.com/library/weekly/aa112099.htm
- www.fieldbook.com/Study_groups/studygroupsHow.html
- www.willamette.edu/cla/ler/studygroups.htm

Working with a Study Buddy

By making yourself understood, listening carefully, and working with your learning style and that of your partner, you will get more out of studying with a study pal. And you will have more fun, too!

You will probably feel a lot less pressure in school if you have someone to work with. When you work with a partner, you have someone to bounce ideas off of, discuss things with, and ask questions of. Here's how a study buddy can help:

- If you are working on the same problem, one of you might know the answer and can help the other; if neither of you knows it, you can figure it out together.

- If you are not working on the same thing, your partner can ask you questions to help you focus your studying. Your partner can also quiz you on the material and help you pinpoint your weak areas. And, of course, you can do the same for him or her.

Two Heads Are Better than One

Jack: What a waste of time. I don't know why the sociology teacher showed us that movie. Nothing really happened in it.

Jill: I disagree. I was really impressed by the way the people in the village stuck together and the way they treated their children.

Jack: That's true. I was surprised. You'd think those kids would be spoiled by all that affection, but it was just the opposite. They really cared about each other. I guess that's why the instructor showed it. But it was still too long.

Jill: I didn't understand the part about the government workers coming to the village. Why couldn't they just leave the villagers alone?

Jack: I kind of liked that part; there was more action, with the trucks coming in and the villagers protesting. I guess it had something to do with the government trying to change the economy, trying to help the villagers get regular jobs instead of digging for roots.

Jill: I hadn't thought about that. That makes sense.

What happened here? Both Jack and Jill saw the film a little differently after reflecting and discussing. Jack began to make more sense of the human issues in the film, and Jill began to make more sense of the political ones. By working together, they made sense of something that was puzzling at first. They figured out much more than they would have if they had been working separately.

Getting Started

You may not be aware of it, but you already know how to work with a study buddy. Whenever you discuss an event, film, or newspaper or magazine article with a friend, you are "working" with a buddy. If you saw the film or read the article, your friend might ask, "What did you think about it?," maybe adding, "I heard it was . . .," or, "I've been meaning to see it myself." Your friend is helping you remember what you saw, heard, or read by asking you that general question.

As you think back on the film or event in order to tell your friend about it, you might think about it a little differently than you did when you saw it. Because your subconscious has had some time to pull it together, you are more apt to have a clearer opinion of it now. Your modified thoughts were triggered by your friend's questions. However, the goal of working with a buddy isn't to change someone's mind, but to help that person be more aware of what he or she is really feeling and thinking.

Finding the Right Study Buddy

Your ideal study buddy should be someone who:

- you are comfortable with
- is responsible and will keep agreements and appointments
- takes learning seriously
- takes you seriously

You may think that your best friend or closest family member will be your best study buddy, and that might be true some of the time. For instance, if you are terribly intimidated by the material you are studying and your best friend or younger sister is the kind of person who gives you the confidence you need to do well, this person may indeed be the best study buddy you could possibly have.

But there are drawbacks to working with someone you know well. You might be tempted to spend your study sessions talking about things other than the topic at hand, which means you might not get much studying done. If you study with someone you barely know, you have less to talk about and are more likely to stay focused on the study material. Whomever you decide to work with, make sure you use study sessions for their purpose: to learn the material, prepare for a test, or complete an assignment.

Setting up a Time and Place

It's important for you and your study buddy to meet fairly regularly. Try an hour per week to start. Decide together what days of the week and times are best for both of you. Decide where you would like to meet. You could take turns going to each other's homes. Some libraries have meeting rooms that you can reserve ahead of time; such neutral territory might be the ideal place to keep you focused. Does your school allow students in the cafeteria after school? This area may work well for study buddies who have an hour to spend between school and track practice. Is there a quiet coffee shop nearby? You want a place that is free of distractions and convenient for both of you.

Getting the Most from Your Study Buddy

Here are some tips for how you and your study buddy can work together.

Set an Agenda

The first thing you and your study buddy have to decide is how long your session will be and what you want to cover in that time. Be realistic when you do this; don't try to cover fifty pages of your textbook in an hour. You may also want to set aside specific portions of your time for special purposes, such as the following:

- *At the beginning:* Allot five minutes for sharing news of the day or airing complaints. If you set aside a specific time period for talking about yesterday's math test or what a lousy day you had, you won't be tempted to spend any more time on it during the rest of your session.

- *At the end:* Allot five to ten minutes at the end for reviewing what you have just learned. Spending time reviewing will help you solidify what you learned and clarify what you still need to work on.

Use Your Time Together Well

Here are some things you and your study buddy can do to help each other understand the material:

- Explain to each other what you already know.
- Help each other find out what you don't know.
- Ask each other questions.
- Help each other find the answers.
- Make connections between what you have just learned and what you already knew.
- Give feedback in preparation for an essay or in-class speech.

Adapt to Each Other's Learning Styles

- *If you learn best by seeing:* As a visual learner, you might have trouble learning when you have to use your ears. Keep notes diligently. When your study buddy makes an interesting point, write it down. Keeping a log of study sessions will help refresh your memory before a test.

- *If you learn best by hearing:* Maybe you think more clearly when speaking. Dictate what you want to say in the written assignment you have to complete and have your buddy act as your secretary. It's important that he or she write down exactly what you say.

MINDBENDER

Put Your Heads Together. You and a study partner can combine your strengths to figure out this mental puzzle.

- Read the problem together; there is no missing information.
- Ask each other questions to clearly understand the problem.
- Brainstorm possible solutions.
- Determine which solution(s) might work.

Problem: You have an old-fashioned refrigerator with a small freezer compartment that can hold at most seven ice cube trays stacked vertically. There are no shelves to separate the trays. You have a dozen trays, each of which can make a dozen cubes, but if you stand one on top of another before it has frozen, it will nest part way into the lower tray, and you won't get full cubes from the lower tray. What is the fastest way to make the most ice cubes?

Solution: *By using frozen cubes as spacers to hold the trays apart, you can make 84 cubes in the time it takes to freeze two trays. Fill one tray, freeze it, and remove the cubes. Place two cubes in the opposite corners of six trays, and fill the rest with water. Freeze all six, plus a seventh you put on top, at the same time. (Note: There are other solutions if you introduce other materials, such as pieces of cardboard large enough to prevent nesting between the trays.)*

STUDY GROUPS

Ned remarks, "In our AP history class, Mr. Silkowski divided us into study groups of four. It was great, because we voted to divide and conquer our long list of history biographies."

Karen says, "My two physical science lab partners and I chose to form a study group to help us review for tests."

Group discussions get everyone involved, but in order for study groups to work well, each person needs to focus on the topic at hand, speak within time limits, listen carefully, and respect others' opinions. You will want to set some ground rules.

Ground Rules for Group Study

1. **Be prepared.** Keep up with your assignments. Your group relies on each member's opinions and interpretations.

2. **Speak up when it's your turn.** If you are nervous about speaking, take a deep breath. Remind yourself that you are with students who are very similar to you. The more you speak, the less nervous you will be.

3. **Help your group keep going.** Whether your instructor has students take turns leading each group or you are all on your own, the group needs participation from everyone in it. Be prepared to coax someone who is shy. If someone is reluctant to speak, ask, "How do you feel about this?" or "Do you agree with . . . ?"

4. **Start with a positive point before criticizing.** Show respect for each other's opinions and feelings. Speak with sensitivity and keep an open mind.

5. **Listen carefully.** When it is someone else's turn, you might want to take notes, which will help you keep track of all ideas and comments. If you are confused by what someone said, say what you thought you heard and follow that up with, "Is that what you meant?"

6. **Appreciate each other's learning styles.** Remember, you all probably learn and teach in different styles—that's a good thing!

7. **Stay within the time limit.** Stay within your time limit if one is assigned. If not, it is simply good manners to give everyone a chance to speak. Also, there should be time at the end of discussion for the group to come to a conclusion.

Check Your Assumptions at the Door!

Exercise your reasoning muscles in your study group with some fun *lateral thinking puzzles*. Lateral thinking puzzles are often strange situations that require an explanation. They are solved through a dialogue between the quizmaster, who knows the puzzle and its solution, and the solvers, who try to figure out the answer. (Pick a new quizmaster for each problem.)

The puzzles, as stated, generally do not contain sufficient information for the solvers to uncover the solution. A key part of the process, therefore, is *asking questions*. The questions can receive one of only three possible answers: "Yes," "No," or "Irrelevant."

When one line of inquiry reaches its end, another approach is needed, often from a completely new direction. This is where the lateral thinking comes in. Some people find it frustrating that for any puzzle it is possible to construct various answers that fit the initial statement of the puzzle. However, for a good lateral thinking puzzle, the "proper" answer will be *the most apt and satisfying*. When you hear the right answer to a good puzzle of this type, you should want to kick yourself for not working it out!

This kind of puzzle teaches you to check your assumptions about any situation. You need to be open-minded, flexible, and creative in your questioning. You may need to put lots of different clues and pieces of information together. Once you reach a viable solution, you have to keep going in order to refine it or replace it with a better solution. This is lateral thinking!

Puzzles

A: The Man in the Elevator. A man lives on the tenth floor of a building. Every day, he takes the elevator down to the ground floor to go to work or to shop. When he returns, he takes the elevator to the seventh floor and walks up the stairs to reach his apartment on the tenth floor. He hates walking, so why does he do it?

B: The Carrot. Five pieces of coal, a carrot, and a scarf are lying on the lawn. Nobody put them on the lawn, but there is a perfectly logical reason why they are there. What is it?

C: Trouble with Sons. A woman had two sons who were born on the same hour of the same day of the same year. They were not twins, and they were not adopted. How can this be true?

Answers

A: *This is a classic puzzle! The man is a midget or a dwarf; therefore, he can't reach the button for the tenth floor. Variants of this puzzle include the clue that, on rainy days, he goes up to the tenth floor in the elevator (because he uses his umbrella!).*

B: *They were used by children who made a snowman. The snow has now melted.*

C: *They were two of a set of triplets (or quadruplets, etc.) This simple puzzle stumps many people. They try outlandish solutions involving test-tube babies or surrogate mothers. Why does the brain search for complex solutions when there is a simpler one available?*

Just the Facts

- Be an *active* listener, absorbing, analyzing, organizing, and recording necessary information.
- Translate what you hear into *useful* notes.
- If needed, ask for help as soon as you can.
- Enjoy the advantages of working with a study buddy or in a study group.

MASTERING THE MATERIALS

Everyone knew Michael was an exceptional student, but Rosa wanted to know *why*. She didn't feel that she could question Michael—she barely knew him. So, Rosa dedicated herself to studying Michael in their history class. She was surprised to see that Michael spent much less time taking notes than she did. Why was that? Rosa wrote nonstop during class and still couldn't capture every thing her teacher said.

When Rosa missed class one day, she saw an opportunity. The following day, she borrowed Michael's class notes to catch up. Rosa discovered that Michael took about one-third the notes she did. And where Rosa's notes were pages of clean handwriting, Michael's notes had arrows pointing to circles containing only a few words. He drew a special box on each page where he listed words to look up. He sometimes drew timelines. He made lists and added stars next to some items.

Rosa asked Michael why he took such funny-looking notes. He explained that much of his class time was spent weighing the information their teacher was giving and deciding how it fit into the overall picture. Michael's goals were to have only the most important items in his notes and to highlight them with graphics, which helped him remember.

Was Rosa or Michael the better note taker?

If you answered "not necessarily Michael," you are right. Michael's visual and graphic techniques obviously work very well for him and maybe for Rosa, too, but they might not suit every student. As you learned in Secret #5, people have different ways of absorbing information and mastering the materials. Let's start with reading.

READING THE MATERIALS

You have made it this far in the book, so it's obvious you can read. But maybe you would like to *master* reading, learning some of the tricks and techniques to get more out of your reading.

The difference between a good reader and a frustrated reader might be the same as the difference between an athlete and a sports fan: One, the athlete, *actively* participates in the sport while the other, the fan, remains on the sidelines. Many people mistake reading for a passive "sideline" task, something that doesn't require active participation. This misconception is a reason why many readers have difficulty understanding and remembering what they read.

If you bought or borrowed this book, chances are you fall into the active or wannabe active category. If so, perhaps the most important thing you can to do improve your reading skills is to become an active reader. This doesn't mean you should work up a sweat while reading, but it does mean that you should be actively involved with the text you are reading. Here are some strategies for doing just that:

- **Skim ahead (preview).**
  Before you read a chapter, read the opening summary or goals, and then skim ahead. Go through and look at the headings or divisions of the chapter. How is it broken down? What are the main topics in that chapter, and in what order are they covered? If the text isn't divided, read the first few words of each paragraph or random paragraphs. What are these paragraphs about? Scan the figure captions. Finally, what key words or phrases are highlighted, underlined, boxed, or bulleted?

  You may not realize it, but subconsciously, your mind picks up a lot. When you skim ahead, the key words and ideas you come across will register in your brain. Then, when you read the information more carefully, there's already a place for that information to go.

- **Jump back (review).**
  When you finish a chapter or a section, jump back. In this book, you are provided with a review at the end of each chapter called "Just the Facts," which provides a summary of important points,

but you should also go back and review the highlights of each section when you have finished. Look back at the headings, the information in bullets, and any information that is otherwise highlighted to show that it is important.

You can jump back at any time in the reading process, and you should do it any time you feel that the information is starting to overload. Skimming ahead and jumping back can also remind you of how what you are reading now fits into the bigger picture. This also helps you better understand and remember what you read because it allows you to make connections and place that information in context. When facts and ideas are related to other facts and ideas, you are far more likely to remember them.

Learn more about memory strategies in Secret #9, Tackling Memory Tricks.

- **Ask questions.**
In any text you read, certain things happen, and they happen for a reason. To find out why they happened, and, more importantly, why it matters, you need to first establish the facts. Like a detective at the scene of a crime, you need to answer some basic questions: *What* happened? *Who* (or *what* was) involved? *When* did it happen? *Where*? *Why*? And *How*?

Once you establish the facts, you can go on to answer the most difficult question: *What does it all add up to? What is the writer trying to show or prove?*

- **Get involved.**
You can make more sense of what you are reading when you get involved with it. And you can do this by anticipating what you read *before* you begin. While you read, ask questions, make pictures in your head, take notes, and use your learning styles.

Here's a hard but not surprising truth: *Reading is work.* It can be easy and enjoyable work, like reading a good story or the comics. Or, it can be more challenging work, such as reading a textbook or other study material.

Now, think a minute about work. If you show up at your job and just sit there till quitting time, did you work? No. You put in your time, but you didn't work. It's the same with reading. If you just sit there moving your eyes over the page, you aren't really reading—and you are not getting much out of it. To get the most out of what you read, your mind should be working before, while, and after you read.

TAKE ADVANTAGE OF THE GRAPHICS

Graphics are pictures, photos, charts, maps, tables, timelines, and other visual ways of representing ideas and data. If what you are reading has graphics, examine them before and during your reading. Ask yourself several questions:

- What do these graphics seem to be about? (Look at titles, captions, and labels.)
- How do they connect with the title or subheads of this chapter?
- How do they improve the text?

WORK THROUGH ALL PROBLEMS

In a math or science book, an author may insert a practice problem to show how a specific theory works in practice. On an exam, you might be expected to know both the theory and how to apply it.

According to *Study Smarts* by Kesselman-Turkel and Peterson, a physics teacher suggests working through all sample problems and proofs:

> Study each sample problem or proof that you come to until you're confident that you understand it. Then close the book and work that problem through from memory. If you get stuck, check it against the book; then wait a while and do it again. Usually these examples are the only problems for which you have a detailed, worked-out solution against which you can check.
> —Judi Kesselman-Turkel and Franklynn Peterson, *Study Smart*,
> Contemporary Books, 1981, Chicago, IL

The authors also suggest that if you are stuck on a sample problem because of complex numbers, try substituting simpler numbers. If you make a mistake, redo the entire problem—you will learn and remember much more that way.

MINDBENDER

Chains of Causes. In your reading, you will have to understand cause-and-effect relationships. For example, a sentence may have the form "A caused B and B caused C": *Jennifer ran a marathon, which made her very tired, so she went to bed early.*
When you analyze this sentence, you can identify two relationships.

Relationship 1: *Jennifer ran a marathon, which made her very tired.*

Relationship 2: *Jennifer was very tired, so she went to bed early.*

Each of the following sentences shows two cause-and-effect relationships. Can you identify them?

1. Robert worked in the sun, which made him very thirsty, so he drank a quart of water.
   Relationship 1: _____
   Relationship 2: _____

2. Judith used her dictionary regularly, which increased her word power, so she scored high on the SAT exam.
   Relationship 1: _____
   Relationship 2: _____

3. Pericles was elected the leader of Athens for 30 years because his ability and honesty earned him the confidence of the people.
   Relationship 1: _____
   Relationship 2: _____

HIGHLIGHTING

Highlighting is using highlighters to mark up your textbook, test preparation books, and notes. Marking the material helps you focus on the most important aspects and skip over the material you know well or don't need to know for the exam. Highlighting words, phrases, and facts will help you see and retain them.

Benefits of Highlighting

- It requires you to make decisions about what is important.
- It focuses your attention on important material.
- It encourages you to spend more time with the material.
- It improves your recall of the highlighted material.

The key to effective highlighting is to be *selective*. If you highlight every other word or sentence, you defeat the purpose. Too many words will be highlighted and nothing will stand out.

So, how do you know what's important enough to highlight? Part of the process is to simply rely on your judgment and to practice. Here are some tips:

- Look for **boldfaced** and *italicized* terms and definitions.
- Consider outlines, bulleted and numbered items, and sidebars.
- Ask two questions: Which facts seem to be emphasized? Which facts are repeated?
- If possible, compare textbook material with the material that is found on practice tests or online tests. If you find that a topic is addressed on several practice tests, you can be sure that the topic warrants highlighting.

What about marking with more than one color? Tina uses a different color highlighter for different subjects. Sammy uses one color to highlight key terms and definitions and another color to highlight procedures. Some people find that using too many colors is cumbersome, but others prefer a variety.

TAKING NOTES

Did you know that just the act of **taking notes**, even if you were never to read them again, will get you higher grades on tests than just listening? That is because taking notes is a muscle activity, and using muscles helps us remember! (People experience this when they drive a stick shift without really thinking about it.)

Good note taking is an art! Like highlighting, the secret to taking good notes is knowing what is important and what is not. Four things that are important enough to record, especially when listening to a lecture, are:

1. main ideas and secondary ideas

2. authorities

3. opinions and facts

4. key terms

When you are sitting in class, listen closely for *main ideas*, or points. Learn to separate them from *secondary*, or supporting, points. A good lecturer will identify main points for you, but sometimes you have to do this on your own. Here are some verbal clues that point toward a main or essential idea:

the reason is. . .

an important factor. . .

there are four things to consider. . .

the thing to remember. . .

the best (or worst, biggest, smallest, last, only, and so on). . .

Secondary ideas are often buried within examples, so be alert to this fact when an instructor offers an example, especially one that follows something you have identified as a main point.

Other details worth recording in your notes are authorities. *Authorities* are experts, research studies, journals, and other sources that lend weight to concepts and facts. A careful student writes down the ideas brought to light, but also notes if this material comes from an authority.

You should also note opinions and facts. *Facts* are bits of information that are real or true. They are generally provable, demonstrable pieces of information. In contrast, *opinions* are beliefs or conclusions held by someone; they may not be objective or proven yet. It may be your opinion that facts are more important than opinions, but this is not necessarily so! An opinion on the future of genetic coding coming from the mouth of the world's most prominent genetic scientist, for example, would have great value. Be sure you identify and separate what is opinion and what is fact in your notes. And any time you don't understand or don't accept a fact or opinion, be sure to put a question mark in your notes, so you can follow up on this point later.

Finally, you will probably hear *key terms*—words, names, or phrases—that are unfamiliar. Write down new vocabulary words with their definitions, if given. Some terms may be defined for you by the instructor, and some you may guess from context. *Context* is how a term is used in a sentence, how it works with the other words and ideas that surround it. If you do not have a definition for a term, be sure to ask about it or put a star next to it in your notes to remind yourself to look it up later.

Where to Write Your Notes

Remember, you are an *active* student, so be prepared—carry whatever you use to write your notes with you!

- **Notebooks.** Carry a notebook with you and write down what you just learned.

- **Address Books.** Use an inexpensive address book to create your own categories in alphabetical order. For example, list the elements of the Periodic Table alphabetically, under their abbreviations. Or create a do-it-yourself dictionary. Alphabetize an unfamiliar word when you come across one, along with your best guess of its meaning (based on context or root word). Later, add the official definition from a dictionary and compare the two.

- **Index Cards.** Jot down anything you want to remember—French vocabulary, chemistry terms, mathematical equations, whatever—each on its own card. Flip through the cards in the car or on the bus to review. More on flashcards later in this chapter.

Rewriting Your Notes

Reorganizing and **rewriting** your notes gives you a chance to review materials and recognize the most significant points. When writing down notes in class, you may not be good at listening, or you may not notice which points are important because you feel rushed. In a review of your notes, the crucial ideas and facts are more likely to surface because you have heard the material once before.

Another benefit of rewriting your notes is that you can write them more legibly the second time.

STUDY AEROBICS

How to SCORE When Rewriting Notes

Select	Choose the most important information from your notes. Don't copy your notes verbatim.
Condense	Shorten long paragraphs or lists by writing a brief summary of the material covered.
Organize	Create headings and subheadings; rearrange the material in your notes more logically; draw a map or timeline.
Rephrase	Use your own words as much as possible; rephrasing helps you re-absorb information.
Evaluate	Decide if your notes are lacking on a particular topic, then ask a classmate if you can share notes.

BE A COPY CAT

If you are learning something complex from a pamphlet or book, choose a few paragraphs you feel are most challenging. Copy them exactly, and then read them out loud. Copy them a second time, and then read them aloud again. Copy a third time; read aloud a third time. This really works!

MAPPING AND DOODLING

Mapping and **doodling** are visual ways to take notes. You can map or doodle information about anything you are studying, whether you are in a classroom listening to a lecture or sitting in the library reading. If you enjoy visualizing, this is a good study strategy for you because the process of drawing a map or doodling a picture can make relationships between topics become clearly visible.

The good news is that you don't have to be an artist to doodle or draw an effective map of information. The process is really straight-forward.

Mapping

In the middle of a clean piece of paper, write down the main point, idea, or topic under consideration. Draw a circle around this main topic. Next, draw branches out from the circle on which you can record subtopics and details. Create as many branches as you need—or as many as will fit on your sheet of paper. The figure on page 110 is an example of a simple map; it has only one level of sub-headings.

The level of detail you will include on each map depends on what you want to remember. Perhaps you already know part of a subject thoroughly but can't seem to remember any details about one or two particular subtopics. In that case, you can tailor the map to fit your needs. Consider Nadya, who has studied the seven major United States Civil War battles in the figure on page 110. She is very familiar with five of them: Gettysburg, Shiloh, Fredericksburg, Manassas, and Vicksburg. However, she is having trouble remembering two of them, Antietam and Cold Harbor. The figure on page 111 shows Nadya's map, which includes all seven major battles of the Civil War; in addition, her map includes specific details about the two battles that she has trouble recalling.

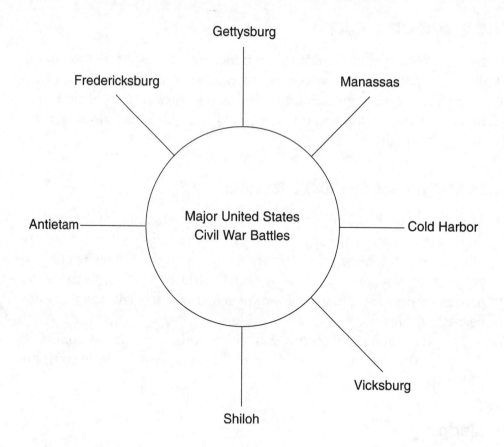

Mapping information forces you to organize the information you are studying, whether that information is from your class notes, a lecture, a field trip, or a textbook. Sometimes you will need to spend considerable time coming up with an appropriate word, phrase, or sentence to write in the center circle of a map. Then you may need to spend even more time considering which topics are related to that main topic for the next level of branches. This process of *making decisions* and *bridging connections* between ideas and facts makes drawing maps an effective study strategy.

Doodling

Doodling, or scribbling notes and pictures, can reflect the speaker's words in a way that will help you absorb a concept, such as a chemical change, or relationships, such as how the various characters in Shakespeare's *A Midsummer Night's Dream* interact.

A further benefit of these graphic strategies is that you end up with an excellent review aid. Because the material is organized in a visual

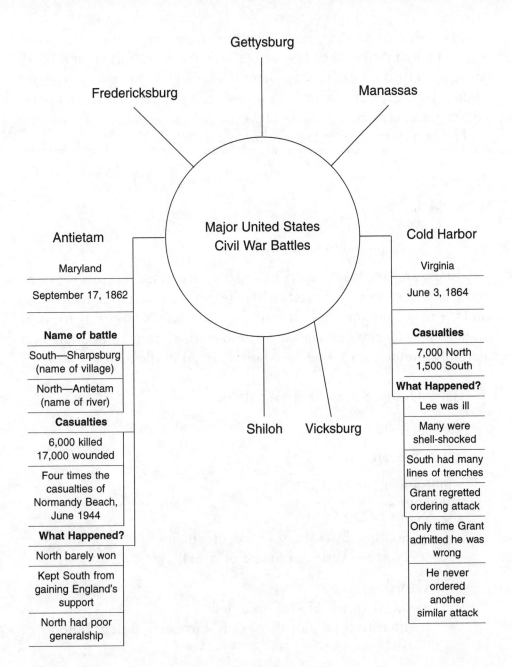

Gettysburg

Fredericksburg

Manassas

Major United States
Civil War Battles

Antietam

Maryland

September 17, 1862

Name of battle

South—Sharpsburg
(name of village)

North—Antietam
(name of river)

Casualties

6,000 killed
17,000 wounded

Four times the
casualties of
Normandy Beach,
June 1944

What Happened?

North barely won

Kept South from
gaining England's
support

North had poor
generalship

Cold Harbor

Virginia

June 3, 1864

Casualties

7,000 North
1,500 South

What Happened?

Lee was ill

Many were
shell-shocked

South had many
lines of trenches

Grant regretted
ordering attack

Only time Grant
admitted he was
wrong

He never
ordered
another
similar attack

Shiloh   Vicksburg

way, you may recall the information more readily each time you review it. It gives the material you are mastering a definite structure, a visual language.

OUTLINING

Outlining is another visual study tool that displays layers of information and how they work together to support the overall main idea.

The outlining strategy is similar to the rewriting-your-notes strategy. The main difference is that outlines are more formal and more structured than notes. That is, there is a certain way in which outlines should be organized. In an outline, you can see exactly how supporting material is related to main ideas.

The basic structure for an outline is this:

1. Topic

   A. Main Idea
      1. Major supporting idea
         a. Minor supporting idea

Outlines can have many layers and many variations, but this is essentially how they work: You start with the topic, move to the main idea, add the major supporting idea, and then list minor supporting ideas (if they seem important enough to write down). Here is an example of a partially completed outline based on material in the map:

1. Major United States Civil War Battles

   A. Antietam

      1. Maryland

      2. September 17, 1862

      3. Name of Battle
         a. South—Sharpsburg (name of village)
         b. North—Antietam (name of river)

      4. Casualties
         a. 6,000 killed; 17,000 wounded
         b. Four times the casualties of Normandy Beach, June 1944

      5. What happened?
         a. North barely won
         b. Kept South from gaining England's support
         c. North had poor generalship

   B. Cold Harbor

      1. Virginia

      2. June 3, 1864

3. Casualties
   a. 7,000 Northerners
   b. 1,500 Southerners

4. What happened?

   a. Lee was ill

   b. Many were shell-shocked

   c. South had many lines of trenches

   d. Grant regretted ordering attack
      1. Only time Grant admitted he was wrong
      2. Never ordered another similar attack

C. Fredericksburg

D. Gettysburg

E. Manassas

F. Shiloh

G. Vicksburg

CATEGORIZING

Let's imagine that Janet has a lengthy list to learn for her geography class: the countries of Africa. She decides to **categorize**—or separate the list into smaller lists, each recognized by a common trait—to make the task more manageable. Janet might organize the nations into these categories:

- geographical sections of Africa
- former colonial status (French, British, Dutch, Belgian, other)
- dates of independence

It is much easier to memorize several small lists than one large one. Organization of information is the key to a large task such as this one.

CREATING YOUR OWN MATERIALS

Here is a list of materials to help you study.

Timelines

In a world history class, for example, you could put large sheets of paper on your bedroom wall to begin timelines. Because you are studying different countries during similar time periods, you could write each country's timeline in a different color. Use the same colors to make notes of events and people in those countries. Or maybe designate a different color for each era—that way you could keep track of what was happening when. If you are using parallel tapes (audio tapes used for similar purposes), categorize them by having one tape for each country or one for each century.

Flashcards

Flashcards or **cue cards** are a popular learning aid. You can get a bit creative with them. Lucia uses different-sized index cards for different subjects: 4×6 for science topics and 3×5 cards for math. Roberta has different colored index cards for various topics, and Timmy writes subcategories in various colored markers. The beauty of index cards is that they are very portable; you can carry them with you throughout the day in your backpack or purse.

Here is an example of a cue card.

the four basic types of chemical reaction	combination decomposition single-displacement (single-replacement) double-displacement (double-replacement)
Front of Card	**Back of Card**

Audio Recording

If one of your learning styles is auditory, try making **audiocassettes** or **CDs** on a recording device. Perhaps you want to record a lecture or simply talk to yourself about new information you are studying, recording your observations and connections.

Two of the main advantages of using cassettes or CDs for reviewing material is that they can be portable and private if you have the right equipment. Listen on the bus or while jogging or waiting in a dentist's office. Tapes and CDs help solidify the material and give greater flexibility and variety to your study plan.

SOURCES IN CYBERSPACE

You will find some great study ideas and tips at these URLs.

- www.readingmatrix.com/reading/reading_texts.html—How to highlight and take margin notes.
- www.mtroyal.ab.ca/CurrentStudents/study_studying.htm—How to study textbooks.
- www.maps.jcu.edu.au/netshare/learn/mindmap/—How to make a mind map (mapping).

Just the Facts

- Be an active reader, skimming ahead, jumping back, and coming up with questions.
- After you read, think back on what you read, looking at the big picture.
- Rework sample problems and proofs and study the explanations.
- Make decisions about what information is important, and then organize it using mastery techniques such as taking notes, highlighting, rewriting, outlining, mapping, categorizing, and doodling.
- Make timeline posters, flashcards, cassettes, and CDs for review, variety, and improved recall.

TACKLING MEMORY TRICKS

In Spanish class, Señora Solis gave Jack a list of vocabulary words to learn. There were Spanish words in one column with the English translations in the other. Jack took the list home and memorized both columns. He put the list on his bedroom mirror, on his refrigerator, in his notebook, and on his TV set. Jack was proud of his efforts and felt he really *knew* those words.

Then came the test. Jack took one look at it and froze. Señora Solis asked for the English translations of the Spanish words Jack had studied. But she changed the order of the words, and Jack had only memorized the list in a certain order. She also asked how some words fit into sentences. Jack couldn't fill in the blanks. He could repeat the exact vocabulary list, but he couldn't translate them at random or use them in a sentence—at least not under the stress of taking a test.

Has Jack really *learned* the words?

What do you think Jack can do to ace his next vocabulary quiz in Spanish class?

Maybe you would suggest these techniques: Jack can make flashcards and review them on the bus, mixing up the cards. He can draw pictures of what the words mean. He can use the words in conversation, substituting one of his new Spanish words when it fits into the context. Jack can sing the words in the shower or rap their meanings while dancing. He can listen for the words on a Spanish TV show or look for them in a Spanish newspaper. He can visualize crazy pictures to link the words on the list together or to link the terms to information he already knows. Hey, Jack, *arriba!*

MEMORIZING AND REMEMBERING

You are studying a lecture or a textbook chapter. You understand it—and now you want it to stick! How do you make sure you won't forget it by tomorrow? The trick is to start by identifying what is important to you and relating it to something you know. Use it in your conversations, write it down, draw it, or record it. Get *actively* involved with the new material, using your preferred learning style (see Secret #5).

Although most students memorize a great deal before a quiz or test, the truth is that straight memorizing is the *least* effective way to remember anything. Better ways to remember facts and formulas are:

1. associating them with something you already know

2. applying multiple senses: hearing, seeing, smelling, touching, speaking

3. drawing or diagramming

4. using mnemonic devices—memory tricks—such as acronyms and acrostics

5. visualizing with methods such as place, peg, and linking

You should know that there is a difference between memorizing something and remembering it. Straight memorization doesn't usually stay with you very long. Real learning, on the other hand, lets you *remember* and *apply* what you learned. Because you use it, it has meaning for you. Because it has meaning for you, you are apt to remember it.

SHORT-TERM AND LONG-TERM MEMORY

There are basically two different kinds of memory, **short-term** and **long-term.** To better understand the difference, think of your brain as a parking facility. One part of it specializes in "parking" new information for only a few days, in short-term parking. If the new information is reinforced in some way, it gets shifted to long-term parking. Attaching new information to an emotion or to another long-term memory are two ways to store new information permanently in this long-term lot. (Researchers believe that most of us can keep between five and nine items at one time in our short-term memories, but we can store an infinite number of items in our long-term memories.)

Let's say you are studying in a chair at the library, reading about cumulus clouds. The girl sitting next to you smells like violets, just like your grandmother, whom you miss terribly. You are likely to remember more about cumulus clouds (even the layout of the page the text was on) because of the emotional attachment your nose and your brain just made. It's true!

As a student, you may learn something at the beginning of the semester that you want to retain for the final exam. For this reason, you will need to move it from short-term memory to long-term memory. You subconsciously do this all the time, especially with something you have an emotional attachment to, such as the memory of picking out your first puppy at the pound.

On the other hand, some things *belong* in short-term memory—they would just clutter up the long-term side. For instance, you learn the Rialto Movie Palace's phone number just long enough to dial up the recording of show times, and then your short-term memory disposes of it.

So, how do you turn short-term memorization into long-term remembering? With the secrets of mnemonics—that's how.

WHAT ARE MNEMONICS ANYWAY?

As a child, did you chant "*i* before *e*, except after *c*"? Do you still? If so, you will probably never forget how to spell "brief" or "receive." **Mnemonics** are memory tricks that can help us to remember what we need to know. *Rhyming*, such as "*i* before *e*, except after *c*," is one kind of mnemonic device. This chapter highlights several specific mnemonic devices so you can:

- file and retrieve important information for upcoming exams
- apply what you learn to how you live
- enjoy learning for its own satisfaction and share it with others

Besides *rhymes and songs*, two popular mnemonic devices that you may have already tried are *acronyms* and *acrostics*. Other memory secrets include *chunking* and visualization techniques such as the *place* and *peg methods* and *linking*. All of these memory devices are designed to help you store, retain, and recall information.

Now, let's take a closer look at some mnemonic tricks.

ACRONYMS

Acronyms are formed by using the first letter from a group of words to form a new word. This is particularly useful when remembering words in a specified order. Acronyms are very common in ordinary language and in many fields. Examples include SCUBA (**S**elf **C**ontained **U**nderwater **B**reathing **A**pparatus) and LASER (**L**ight **A**mplification by **S**timulated **E**mission of **R**adiation). What other common acronyms can you think of?

Your geography teacher wants you to learn the names of the Great Lakes. You might make the acronym HOMES, which is a word formed by the first letter from each of the names of the Great Lakes:

Huron

Ontario

Michigan

Erie

Superior

"Homes" is a real word; however, you can also make up a nonsense word to help you remember a list. A common acronym for reviewing the colors of the visible spectrum is the silly word "roygbiv." You can turn this into an imaginary person's name, "Roy G. Biv," if that helps you remember the letters.

Red

Orange

Yellow

Green

Blue

Indigo

Violet

Note: In this case—and in contrast with the Great Lakes example— the *order* of the items to be remembered (colors) is essential because this is their order in the spectrum.

Now, consider the acronym NIMBY, often heard in city council and planning board meetings. NIMBY refers to people who protest the construction of, say, a power plant in their neighborhood. This acronym stands for an entire phrase: "Not In My Back Yard!" As you can see, some acronyms stand for words or phrases that have to be in a certain order, and some do not.

An interesting twist on acronyms is one named for a real person, Dr. Virginia Apgar, the American anesthesiologist who designed the index for rating newborn babies. Healthcare professionals often remember the assessment for newborns this way:

Appearance (color)

Pulse

Grimace (response to stimuli)

Activity (muscle tone)

Respiration

Although acronyms can be very useful memory aids, they do have some disadvantages. First, they are useful for rote memory but do not aid comprehension. Be sure to differentiate between comprehension and memory, keeping in mind that understanding is often the best way to remember. Some people assume that if they can remember something, they must "know" it, but as we saw in Jack's case, memorization does not necessarily lead to understanding.

A second problem with acronyms is that they can be difficult to form; not all lists of words will lend themselves equally well to this technique. Finally, acronyms, like everything else, can be forgotten if not committed to memory.

Creating Acronyms

Since you can create an acronym for just about anything you want to remember, you can use acronyms to help you recall the material you are studying for just about any quiz or test. Even though it will take you a few minutes to create an acronym, the extra effort pays off during exam time when you are able to retrieve crucial information.

Follow these steps to create your own acronyms:

1. Choose a particular list of terms you want to memorize or a number of steps in a process you want to be able to recall.

2. Write down those terms or steps on a sheet of paper.

3. If the order of the terms or steps is not essential, consider rearranging the terms.

4. Be creative in finding one or more words that consist of the first letters of the terms or steps in your list.

5. Pick the acronym from your brainstorming that you are most likely to remember based on your own experience, memory, and knowledge. CLUE: *Link what you know to what you need to remember.*

6. Arrange the terms you want to recall in the order of your chosen acronym. Highlight or underscore the first letter of each term so when you review, it will be easier to see the acronym.

Once you invest the time in creating acronyms, review them often. You can rewrite them or read them aloud. Study your acronyms over and over until they become familiar friends. The same may be said for *acrostics.*

ACROSTICS

Another type of mnemonic is a silly sentence or phrase, known as an **acrostic**, which is made of words that each begin with the letter or letters that start each item in a series you want to remember. For example, "Please Excuse My Dear Aunt Sally" is a nonsensical acrostic that math students use to remember the order of operations:

Please **E**xcuse **M**y **D**ear **A**unt **S**ally =
Parentheses, **E**xponents, **M**ultiply, **D**ivide, **A**dd, **S**ubtract

Here's another example of an acrostic. To remember the letters of the notes on the lines of the treble clef (E, G, B, D, and F), music students often recite this acrostic: **E**very **G**ood **B**oy **D**oes **F**ine. (The notes on the spaces between the lines form the acronym **FACE** for the musical notes F, A, C, and E.) Can you think of other examples?

Like acronyms, acrostics can be very simple to remember and are particularly helpful when you need to remember a list in a specific order. One advantage of acrostics over acronyms is that they are less limiting; if your words don't form easy-to-remember acronyms, using acrostics may be preferable. On the other hand, they can take more thought to create and require remembering a whole new sentence rather than just one word. Otherwise, they present the same problem as acronyms in that they aid memorization but not comprehension.

Elaborate Acrostics

Some word-loving people make up very elaborate acrostics, even using more letters than the first letter of each word. Lyla invented this amazing acrostic to recall the five phases of mitosis in biology (metaphase, prophase, prometaphase, anaphase, telophase):

METAman **PRO**posed **PRO**fusely to **ANA** on the **TELO**phone!

METAphase

PROphase

PROmetaphase

ANAphase

TELOphase

Can you see that the following clever acrostic reminds us how to move up the scale of metric prefixes, from the basic unit to larger units?

Decadent Hector Killed Meg's Gigantic Terrier!

Decadent	**Deca**	10
Hector	**Hecto**	10^2
Killed	**Kilo**	10^3
Meg's	**Mega**	10^6
Gigantic	**Giga**	10^9
Terrier	**Tera**	10^{12}

Remember that you will have an easier time memorizing an acronym or an acrostic that you can identify with, are interested in, or that you find humorous. So, take the time you need to come up with something memorable. Why don't you give it a whirl? Invent an acronym or an acrostic for these seven mnemonic devices: acronym, acrostic, rhyming, chunking, linking, place, peg.

RHYMES AND SONGS

Janine writes in her lecture notes "A pint's a pound the world around," a rhyme that will remind her that a pint of water weighs one pound when test time comes around! **Rhythm, repetition, melody,** and **rhyme** can all aid memory. Do you remember these favorite learning rhymes? Did you learn any others?

- In 1492, Columbus sailed the ocean blue.
- Thirty days hath September, April, June, and November.

Are you familiar with Homer's *Odyssey*? If so, you know that the epic is very long. That is why it is so remarkable that the *Odyssey*, along with many ancient stories, was related by storytellers who relied solely on their memories. Even in modern Africa, family historians called *griots* recite hundreds of years of ancestors' names from memory! The use of rhyme, rhythm, and repetition are essential to these ancient and modern storytellers.

As a child, you probably learned your ABCs to the tune of "Twinkle, Twinkle, Little Star." We have even heard of one algebra student who demonstrated how she memorized the quadratic formula (notorious for being long and difficult to remember) by singing it to a familiar tune!

Using these techniques can be fun, particularly for people who like to create. Rhymes and songs draw upon your auditory memory and may be particularly useful for those who can learn tunes, songs, or poems easily.

CHUNKING

Chunking is a technique used to group or "chunk" items—generally numbers—together for better recall, although the process can be used for recalling other things too. It is based on the concept, mentioned earlier, that the average person can store about seven items (plus or minus two) in his or her short-term memory. Have you noticed how many digits local phone numbers have these days?

When you use chunking, you decrease the number of items you are holding in your memory by increasing the size of each item. For example, to recall the number string 10301988, you could try to remember each number individually, or you could try thinking about the string as 10 30 19 88 (four chunks of numbers). Instead of remembering eight individual numbers, you are remembering four larger numbers, right?

As with acronyms and acrostics, chunking is particularly meaningful when chunking has a personal connection. In our number string, Karl might make two chunks, 1030 and 1988, because he sees that the first chunk is the last four digits of his zip code and the second is his sister's birth year.

Go Ahead—Play with Your Words!

Word games—such as puns, spoonerisms, and quips—can help you remember facts, as well as "limber up" your brain. For instance, when you need to memorize vocabulary or names, you can make a play on words that will attach the word or name to your long-term memory. Some examples follow.

1. To remember the word *pessimist*, make a pun: *A pessimist's blood type is always B negative.*

2. To recall what *egotist* means, put it in a playful context: *When two egotists meet, it's an I for an I.*

3. To remember what the scientist Pavlov did, make a quip: *Does the name Pavlov ring a bell?*

THE POWER OF VISUALIZATION

One powerful way to make a strong connection between facts and long-term memory is to visualize, or create pictures of, what you want to learn. Remember, *you will understand and retain new information more readily if you creatively connect new, unfamiliar material to something that is already familiar to you.* Think of these connections as individual strings tying each new fact or idea down in your brain. When you make several connections to a fact or idea, you create several strings to tie it down in your mind. Since one string can be easily broken, the more connections you make, the better. You want to create enough strings to firmly anchor information in your memory. (By the way, you just used visualization to absorb a concept!)

The key to making strong connections is to create vivid mental pictures of each specific incident that relates to each term (or fact or formula) you want to recall. Here's what to do:

1. Spend a few minutes with your eyes closed, thinking about each term, to create a strong mental image.

2. Fill in the details in your mind's eye.

3. Involve as many senses as possible to create truly memorable connections.

You may find that this strategy works better when you use it to study and recall main ideas, rather than smaller details about a topic. That's because the more detailed the information you want to recall, the less likely you are to know of a specific case you can connect it to in your own experience. Using the steps listed earlier, you could create mental images of past events to remember the four ways that poisons enter the body.

However, to recall more detailed information about poisons, you may want to employ another study strategy. For instance, you could use flashcards to learn how a first aid worker can reduce absorption of a poison (induce vomiting using syrup of ipecac, pump the stomach, or administer activated charcoal). In other words, you can mix strategies—whatever works for you.

Harnessing the power of visualization helps you be creative when thinking about your study material. Now, let's examine three additional memory techniques where visualization plays a vital role: the place and peg methods and linking.

THE PLACE METHOD

One of the oldest mnemonics that is still in use today is called the *method of loci*, which was first recorded over 2,500 years ago. This technique was used by ancient orators to remember speeches, and it combines the use of organization, visual memory, and association. Today it is often called the **place method**. The first step in using the place method is to think about a place you know very well, perhaps your living room or bedroom. Think of a location that has several pieces of furniture or other large items that always remain in the same place. These items become your *landmarks* or *anchors* in the place method mnemonic. The number of landmarks you choose will depend on the number of things you want to remember.

You need to know where each landmark is in the room, and when you visualize walking around this room, you must always walk in the same direction (an easy way to be consistent is to always move around the room in a clockwise direction or from the door to the opposite wall). What is essential is that you have a vivid visual memory of the path and objects along it.

The next step is to assign an item that you want to memorize to each landmark in your room. An effective technique is to visualize each word literally attached to each landmark. Here's an example of how one physical education student used the place method to remember the nine positions in baseball. This example uses landmarks in the student's bedroom.

Place Method Sample

Landmark Position

1. doorway	→	1. pitcher
2. chair	→	2. catcher
3. TV stand	→	3. first baseman
4. vase with flowers	→	4. second baseman
5. nightstand	→	5. third baseman
6. bed	→	6. shortstop
7. closet	→	7. left fielder
8. bookcase	→	8. center fielder
9. table with skirt	→	9. right fielder

Our student might imagine each baseball position written on or attached to each landmark. Or imagine each player connected to each landmark in some way: The pitcher is blocking the doorway, chewing gum and tossing the ball into his glove, and the second baseman is holding the flower vase with a number 2 on it.

To make the place method work, you must first study and understand each item you want to remember, so you can visualize it and directly link it to the right anchor in your chosen place. The more vivid—even bizarre—your visualization is, the stronger the connection will be between the material and the landmarks that are already entrenched in your memory.

If you have never heard of the place method before, you may want to start asking servers who don't write down their customers' orders how they remember who gets what. You may find that they rely on the place method to keep track of people's orders because it works so well!

STUDY AEROBICS

1. **Repeat after me: "Repetition! Repetition!"** Mnemonic devices require active participation and constant repetition of the material to be memorized. This repetition is not passive; it is meaningful practice. Look at the list, learn the terms, attach

a mnemonic device to them, memorize, duplicate, and check your work. This process acts as a holding pattern while memory links are formed in your brain.

2. **Practice NOT cramming.** Trying frantically to learn all the material you need to know the night before your big exam can frazzle your nerves and leave you too exhausted to do your best. Besides, studies show that cramming does not lead to long-term retention of knowledge.

3. **Review over the long stretch.** Your success depends on reviewing materials often and over long stretches of time. Information memorized quickly, during a single block of time, does not stick in your mind.

THE PEG METHOD

The **peg method** is similar to the place method, but it uses numbers and a poem instead of landmarks to set vital information into long-term memory. An advantage of the peg method over the place method is that you can recall items in any order instead of having to go through the entire sequence to get to one of the items in the middle of the list.

The first step in using the peg method is to memorize this simple poem. You have to know this poem by heart so that you can use the numbers in it to anchor the new information.

One is a bun

Two is a shoe

Three is a tree

Four is a door

Five is a hive

Six is sticks

Seven is heaven

Eight is a gate

Nine is wine

Ten is a hen

The second step is to compile the list of items to remember. Then simply picture the first new term with the first word in the poem (*bun*). Then picture the second word you want to learn with the second word in the poem (*shoe*). For example, you might use the peg method for the names of the nine planets. This table shows how you might attach the first three planets, Mercury, Venus, and Earth, to their peg words from the poem.

Peg Word	Planet
1. bun →	Mercury—Mercury is the hottest planet, so you imagine a baker taking a bun with "Mercury" burned onto it from an oven.
2. shoe →	Venus—Venus is the goddess of love, so you envision her dressed up, in beautiful golden shoes.
3. tree →	Earth—You see our planet, the only one covered in trees.

And so on, through all nine planets, visualizing something you already know about each planet and "hanging" it on the peg. Once again, the more vivid your visualization, the stronger the connection will be.

LINKING

A similar memory trick is **linking,** in which you link each item to the preceding one using flamboyant images. With practice, you should be able to link and recall many items. Let's demonstrate with a short shopping list, noting that the principal works for a long shopping list as well.

1. ketchup

2. ice cream

3. newspaper

4. eggs

5. pork chops

Begin by associating or linking the first item, ketchup, with the store where you shop. Go ahead and do that.

Visualize your market in as much detail as you can. See the front of the building. Are there rows of shopping carts outside? How many doors does the building have? Focus on one doorway.

You must associate a bottle of ketchup with this image. You might see an ordinary bottle of ketchup on the ground outside the doorway, but this is not an image that your memory is likely to latch onto. Try this:

Visualize yourself trying to enter the building but unable to get around whatever is blocking the doorway. What is it? A gigantic bottle of ketchup. How are you going to get in to do your shopping? You'll just have to smash the bottle. See yourself getting a shopping cart and ramming it into the bottle.

Note: It is important to use as many senses as you can. Approximately 65% of us are stimulated visually, 30% audibly, and 5% kinesthetically (by touch). So you must not only see this bottle of ketchup smashing, but also hear the sound of the breaking bottle and smell the ketchup.

Now see all that ketchup oozing out of the bottle, slowly moving toward you like lava, until it finally knocks you over, covering you from head to toe. Feel the ketchup as it slowly engulfs you. Use all your senses. Do you have that image? It is an image that your memory will surely latch onto.

Next, we go to item two on our shopping list, ice cream. We must link this item to the first one, ketchup, in just as silly a way. A normal, logical association may be a bottle of ketchup on a table beside a bowl of ice cream. But that's too normal, too logical.

The ketchup has almost engulfed you, and you take a whiff as it reaches your nose. Hey, this doesn't smell like ketchup, it smells like strawberry ice cream. In fact, it is strawberry ice cream! As you lay on your back, you pluck two ice cream cones from the air, take a scoop with each, and enjoy the ice cream.

Remember, there are no rules—you can imagine and do as you please when linking, just as long as it is ridiculous. Once you have each image firmly in mind, you can let it go. You don't have to consciously associate ketchup with the store's doorway. You don't have to worry about linking ketchup to ice cream. The images will all come to you when you need them. Now, linking *ice cream* to *newspaper*:

You stand up with a cone in each hand. Next to the doorway is a newspaper box. You walk over to it and instead of inserting quarters, you shove one ice cream cone into the slot. The door doesn't open, so you squish the other cone into the slot and the door opens.

Next, we link *newspaper* to *eggs*:

The second you open the newspaper door, hundreds of eggs come flying out like in a cartoon. They hit you in the head, chest, and arms; you duck and they hit people walking behind you. You are covered in yolk and eggshells.

Now, go from *eggs* to *pork chops*:

Just as the last egg has shot out of the box, you tentatively look inside. Suddenly, the huge head of a pig pops out from the newspaper door opening.

He slowly and noisily squeezes himself out and lands on the ground in front of you. This is one big, smelly pig!

That's a sample of five items. Now, forget about these associations and count to 60. The counting forces you to take your mind off of the items on the list. But if you successfully formed the images of the shopping list as described, you will still be able to recall them. Let's prove it.

Now, fill in the five-item shopping list:

1. _____

2. _____

3. _____

4. _____

5. _____

Did one image spark off the next? If you can recall 5 items with this method, you can just as easily recall 15 or 25. The length of the list isn't important. What matters is the strength of each link in the chain. As soon as you form a link between two items that isn't nonsensical, the list may break down.

These sample images are intended to show you just how silly they must be. Your own link between, say, newspaper and eggs will be different. In fact, these links will *always* be stronger if they are your own. Note that linking can be used for memorizing not only lists, but also speeches, instructions, and complex formulas and equations. With practice, linking may become your favorite mnemonic trick.

SOURCES IN CYBERSPACE

Memory Tricks
Check out these URLs for articles on pumping your memory to the max.

- www.dso.iastate.edu/dept/asc/all/study_skills.htm#Memory— Multiple Study Skills links, including note-taking, time-management and stress-management techniques.

- www.kporterfield.com/ld/ld_memory.html—Amazing Memory Tricks for People with Learning Disabilities (applies to every learner).
- www.berkeley.edu/news/media/releases/97legacy/ 10_17_ 97a.html—A fascinating page on how squirrels and birds remember where they hide food.

Just the Facts

- Identify what is important for you to know.
- Pick the best memory device for the materials and for your learning style: rhyme and song, acronyms, acrostics, chunking, visualization, place method, peg method, or linking.
- Make your mnemonic devices as personal and vivid as possible.
- Apply multiple senses when you can.

PREVENTING TEST STRESS

Tan always creates rules for himself, and nowhere is this more obvious than in how he prepares for tests. His sister Phuong teases him about his many rules, but she is secretly adopting some of his techniques.

Phuong used to stay up late studying and then cram until her teacher passed out the test. Now, she follows Tan's rule of studying no later than midnight the night before a test. Phuong routinely skipped breakfast on test days so she could spend more time studying. Now, she makes a point of sitting down and eating a nutritious, unrushed breakfast, as her brother does.

But it is this simple rule that most increases Phuong's peace of mind on test days: *Check that your materials are ready*. Just before she leaves the house, she checks that her backpack has pencils, her notes and textbook, and a sweater (in case the test room gets chilly). Phuong feels calmer knowing that she is prepared.

Phuong's secret was safe until one evening when she was studying for a biology test. She was checking off a to-do list, just like Tan did before a big exam. When she looked up, she saw her brother grinning at her. Phuong expected to be teased; after all, she had done the same to him. But Tan only grinned. "Just keep your hands off my lucky test-taking socks," he said.

If your study techniques leave you anxious on test day, follow Phuong's lead by testing and then adopting the study techniques of other good students. Most of us have at least one friend who always seems to be organized and prepared. Don't be embarrassed to ask such friends for study tips and advice. He or she will probably be flattered and more than willing to help. The proper study and test preparation routine is essential to preventing test stress and anxiety. In this chapter, you will learn how to recognize the symptoms of test stress as well as how to effectively relieve them.

SYMPTOMS OF TEST STRESS

Although you may know the materials, and even though you have read all hints and tips in this book, one factor may still interfere with your ability to successfully function on test day: test stress.

The best way to alleviate test stress is to first recognize your symptoms and gain an understanding that the possible reason for subpar test performance is not lack of intelligence or knowledge, but is directly related to the stress you feel before and during the test.

You may recognize test stress by the jittery feeling you get in the pit of your stomach. Although it may sound like a cliché, your palms may begin to sweat or your mouth may suddenly become dry. The worse symptom of all could be the sudden blank you draw when trying to answer questions that you were able to answer almost automatically when studying with your study buddy. Many times after leaving a test and relaxing a bit, you remember the answers to the question or questions that stumped you the most.

Some symptoms of stress include:

- an increased heart rate
- rapid breathing
- stammering
- headaches and stomachaches
- chest pains
- diarrhea
- sweating
- sleeplessness
- alcohol and drug abuse

Do any of these symptoms sound familiar? If you experience these symptoms on test day, then you may be suffering from test stress.

Are You Stressed?

Now that you have had test stress explained to you, and the symptoms have been pointed out, you can make a determination about the level of test stress you may be experiencing. It is common for all test takers to feel a little nervous on test day, but suffering from test stress is a more severe form of the normal jitters. If you are feeling test stress, you will find that you have already taken one of the first steps to alleviating that stress simply by reading this book and practicing some of the tips found within. You can also unburden yourself of some of this stress by ensuring that you are healthy both mentally and physically.

MINDBENDER

Test-Stress Test

You only need to worry about test anxiety if it is extreme enough to impair your performance. The following questionnaire will provide a diagnosis of your level of test anxiety. In the blank before each statement, write the number that most accurately describes your experience.

0 = Never   1 = Once or twice   2 = Sometimes   3 = Often

_____ I have gotten so nervous before an exam that I put down the books and didn't study for it.

_____ I have experienced disabling physical symptoms such as vomiting and severe headaches because I was nervous about an exam.

_____ I have not shown up for an exam because I was scared to take it.

_____ I have experienced dizziness and disorientation while taking an exam.

_____ I have had trouble filling in the little circles because my hands were shaking too hard.

_____ I have failed an exam because I was too nervous to finish it.

_____ Total: Add up the numbers in the blanks above.

Your Test-Stress Score

Here are the steps you should take, depending on your score. If you scored:

- **Less than 3,** your level of test anxiety is nothing to worry about; it's probably just enough to give you that little extra edge.
- **Between 3 and 6,** your test anxiety may be enough to impair your performance, and you should practice the stress management techniques listed in this section to try to bring your test anxiety down to manageable levels.
- **More than 6,** your level of test anxiety is a serious concern. In addition to practicing the stress management techniques listed in this section, you may want to seek additional personal help. Call your local high school or community college and ask for the academic counselor. Tell the counselor that you have a level of test anxiety that sometimes keeps you from being able to take the exam. The counselor may be willing to help you or may suggest someone else you should talk to.

HEALTHY IN MIND

Being mentally healthy, in this case, does not refer to your growing intellect, but more about your emotional health. Surrounding yourself with positive influences will undoubtedly create a mentally healthy you and that will lead to a healthier and more positive outlook on your everyday life, including that dreaded chemistry exam! Some of the factors that directly affect your mental health include the following.

Your Peer Group

It may be a difficult fact to admit to yourself, but your peer group may be holding you back from performing your best academically. Think of your core group of friends and classmates. Do they share your yearning to do their best in school? Are they supportive of your efforts to study and do well on tests? Unfortunately, some high school students become disengaged from the whole learning experience and actually belittle those around them who strive to do well. On the other hand, surrounding yourself with positive peer influences will provide you with the support necessary to make you feel good about your study efforts.

Personal Environment

Unfortunately, this is something that you may have little control over. It has been found that students who are going through major life situations are more likely to experience stress in their everyday lives. Some of these major life events include:

- the death of a loved one
- divorce
- moving to a new town
- major health issues in the family
- living in a dysfunctional family

It is unfortunate that many high school students must live through these problems, and they do indeed take a toll on their mental health. If you are now experiencing or recently have experienced one of these events, take an honest look at how it is affecting you. If necessary, seek the guidance of a counselor, friend, or role model to help you cope with the many unique issues surrounding your situation.

STUDY AEROBICS

Creating your own anti-anxiety routine: Pay careful attention to your anxiety level throughout the school week and on the weekends. What activities tend to relax you? If, for example, you find that playing basketball or practicing yoga helps you de-stress, be sure to schedule a practice session the morning or night before a major test. By the same token, take note of the activities that tend to make you anxious, and avoid them when you have an impending exam.

What to Do

If you recognize that your mental well-being is not as healthy as it could be, be encouraged to seek the help of a counselor, family physician, friend, or role model.

HEALTHY IN BODY

You may think of test taking as an exercise of the brain, but, in reality, your physical health may also play a role in your ability to perform well academically. There are many factors that can affect your health, and, therefore, your academic success.

During the high school years, teens become ever more conscious of their bodies and physiques. This is perfectly natural because their bodies are undergoing substantial changes as a result of puberty. Unfortunately, this attention to looks and build sometimes leads to unhealthy eating habits if teens become obsessed with maintaining a look that they consider to be most desirable. These unhealthy habits deprive the body of the nutrients necessary to grow, heal, and yes, think.

These years are also the prime years for social outings with friends and classmates. Wherever there are social events, there seems to be food, and often this food is not the most nutritious. Try to be careful with your diet, and maintain a healthy balance between junk food and the healthy food that contains the nutrients your maturing body needs.

WORK

You may be one of the more than 5 million teens who hold jobs while attending high school. You may work out of necessity, but be aware that your part-time job may be taking a toll on your academic success. If you see that your work schedule is keeping you from your studies, it may be time to reassess the value of your job. Sure, the extra spending money may be nice when you go the mall, or you may be saving for a large purchase such as a stereo or a new car, but be sure that you are not carrying the extra cash around at the expense of your education.

If your job is getting in the way of your academics there are many things you can do:

- **Evaluate the pros and cons of keeping the job.**
  Make a list of all the good things that the job provides you, and then make a list of the areas of your life that are detrimentally affected by your job. Which list wins?

- **Discuss your work schedule with your supervisor.**
  Your supervisor may be willing to adjust your work schedule to better fit your academic needs. If you have an important test, such as a

mid-term or a final exam, coming up, be sure to discuss this with your supervisor so that you can have the necessary time off to study and prepare for the exam. Many supervisors will recognize your candor and desire to perform well in school as an admirable trait and will work with you to meet that goal.

- **Discuss work options with your school counselor.**
  If you come to the realization that your current work situation is not the best for you or your academic success, speak with your school counselor. Many schools offer work opportunities that also count toward graduation. Students participating in these programs participate in regular classes during part of the day, and then leave for their jobs at offices, banks, and other places of business for the rest of the day. These jobs often offer real life applications to the things you are learning in school.

EXTRACURRICULAR ACTIVITIES

After school and civic activities provide wonderful learning and social opportunities for teens. It is important that you do not overwhelm yourself with these activities to the point that you are unable to keep up with your studies. Many school systems have checks in place so that students with failing grades are barred from participating in certain activities until they raise their grades to passing levels. Avoid this potentially embarrassing situation by monitoring your participation in extracurriculars yourself. If you see that they are getting in the way of your academic success, you should consider eliminating one or more from your schedule.

SOURCES IN CYBERSPACE

Stress Relief
- www.wisespirit.com/stress.htm—Strategies and exercises for relieving stress.
- www.personalpowercoach.com/dealstressanxiety.htm—Top 10 ways to deal with stress and anxiety.
- www.factsontap.org/commuter/stress.html—Drug- and alcohol-free ways to deal with school stress.

SLEEP

Get your rest! You may start yawning when you realize that research has shown that the average teen needs more than nine hours of sleep per night. Unfortunately, recent studies have shown that teens' sleep needs do not often correlate with their schedules. Chemical changes in the body during the teen years cause most teens to stay up later than they did during childhood. Even a teenager who goes to bed at 9 P.M. is unlikely to settle into sleep at that time. Thus, teens typically want to stay up later simply because their bodies are telling them to stay awake. This would not be a problem if schools did not start until 10 A.M., but most high school students must be at school much earlier than that.

The combination of the physiological changes in teenagers' bodies and the schedules enforced by society mean that most teens are not meeting this nine-hour mark for the sleep their bodies require. This is why many are tired and sometimes lethargic by the time the weekend comes around. You may find that your body wants to sleep late on weekend mornings, but that you are not tired at night and want to spend the late hours of the night socializing with friends, enjoying time with your family, or just spending time with a video game or a good book.

To help your body get the rest it needs, try to set your body's internal clock to its optimum schedule. Make every attempt to establish and keep a regular sleep schedule. If you must, supplement your overnight sleep with short naps after school. Getting the proper amount of sleep not only leaves you feeling refreshed and ready for the day, but it gives your body the downtime it needs to function at its best during your waking hours.

TIPS FOR BEING STRESS-FREE

If you are suffering from test stress, you may want to try some of these stress-relieving tips:

- **Do not create unrealistic or unattainable goals** by telling yourself what you "should" do.
  Just do the best that you can, knowing that you are well prepared for the exam.
- **Get plenty of sleep.**
  Exhaustion decreases ability to cope with stress.

- **Eat balanced meals.**
  Diet and exercise are important for your complete health. Be sure to enjoy nutritious meals on a regular basis.

- **Don't take stimulants.**
  Although sodas are a staple of teen life, and it may be tempting to use chocolate and soda to give yourself that extra boost of energy, these stimulants are only short-lived and do not contribute positively to your overall health.

- **Don't psyche yourself up to fail.**
  Be mentally tough, be confident in your study habits, and enjoy the fruits of your hard work. Do not tell yourself things like "I know I am not going to do well on this test!" These statements often become self-fulfilling prophecies. Instead, be positive in your thoughts, and surround yourself with peers who are equally positive.

- **Study!**
  Nothing will make you feel more stressed than walking into the classroom knowing that you did not review the materials that you are going to be tested on. Whatever it takes, be sure that you review the materials before the test.

- **Reward yourself.**
  Be sure that you reward yourself throughout the entire process. Reward yourself for good study habits, and eventually reward yourself for scoring well on your exams. Setting up a realistic reward system will help you meet your goals and make the study and test cycle seem less burdensome.

- **Practice taking tests.**
  If you have taken practice tests, either those that you have created on your own or those that your study buddy has created for you, you will have gotten over the test jitters prior to actually taking the real test. This preparedness can do nothing but boost your self-confidence on test day.

- **Think positively!**
  This is probably the most important of all the tips. It cannot be repeated enough that you should surround yourself with positive influences and positive thoughts. Challenge yourself to do the best that you can, and do not be afraid to pat yourself on the back for a well-earned score!

- **Do not dwell on the past.**
  Even if you bombed your last biology test, do not walk into the classroom expecting to do the same on this one! Remember that this test is different, and approach it with a fresh outlook.

Just the Facts

- Alleviate test stress by first recognizing the symptoms.
- Be mindful of your emotional as well as physical health.
- Surround yourself with positive influences.
- Maintain a healthy and balanced diet.
- Don't let a part-time job or too many extracurricular activities get in the way of your academic success.
- Get plenty of sleep.

EPILOGUE: TAKE ADVANTAGE OF THE SECRETS!

In your hands, you have the guide to the ten secrets that will help you unlock your potential. Do not hesitate to use them! By exploring, learning, and then utilizing these secrets, you will become a better and more confident test taker, therefore, eliminating your test stress! The ten secrets we uncovered are

- Managing Time and Being Prepared
- Getting a Handle on Objective Testing
- Getting a Handle on Subjective Testing
- Mastering Your Study Environment
- Discovering Your Learning Style
- Creating and Implementing a Study Plan
- Getting the Most out of Class
- Mastering the Materials
- Tackling Memory Tricks
- Preventing Test Stress

Your Guide to State Board of Education Websites

Listed below are the websites for each of the fifty state education departments. When you enter each state website, you will be on the homepage. Follow the links to each website's high school exit exam page.

As you scan your state website, you should also go into any links labeled *Assessment*. Many states display past examinations on their sites for the express purpose of having classroom teachers and students understand exactly what will be tested and how. Look for *Sample Responses*, which often provide a detailed explanation of how each paper was scored. These sample items can be used for test practice, whether at home or in the classroom.

Other important information included on your state website will be the *Report Card* for the state. How did your district do in comparison to other districts in the state? Some states let you access your individual school from the main website. In that case, you can check your school's progress. If the state website does not give your school's information, you can obtain this information from your school district office or the building principal. These documents can be confusing to read at first, so do not hesitate to ask for help. You should know just where your school falls in its yearly testing program.

State Departments of Education

Alabama Teacher Education and Certification Office
State Department of Education
50 North Ripley Street
P.O. Box 302101
Montgomery, AL 36104
334-242-9935
www.alsde.edu

Alaska Department of Education
801 W. 10th Street, Suite 200
Juneau, AK 99801-1894
907-465-2800
www.educ.state.ak.us

Arizona Department of Education
1535 West Jefferson Street
Phoenix, AZ 85007
602-542-4361
800-352-4558
www.ade.state.az.us

Arkansas Department of Education
Four Capitol Mall
Little Rock, AR 72201
501-682-4475
arkedu.state.ar.us

California Department of Education
1430 North Street, Room 5111
Sacramento, CA 95814
916-319-0827
www.cde.ca.gov

Colorado Department of Education
201 E. Colfax Avenue
Denver, CO 80203-1799
303-866-6600
www.cde.state.co.us

Connecticut State Department of Education
165 Capitol Avenue
Hartford, CT 06145
860-713-6548
www.state.ct.us/sde

Delaware Department of Education
John G. Townsend Building
401 Federal Street
P.O. Box 1402
Dover, DE 19903-1402
302-739-4601
www.doe.state.de.us

District of Columbia Teacher Education and Licensure Branch
441 4th Street, NW, Suite 920 North
Washington, DC 20001
202-727-6436
www.washingtondc.gov/citizen/education.htm

Florida Department of Education
Turlington Building
325 West Gaines Street
Tallahassee, FL 32399-0400
850-487-1785
www.firn.edu/doe

Georgia Department of Education
205 Jesse Hill Jr. Drive, SE
Atlanta, GA 30334
404-656-2800
www.doe.k12.ga.us

Hawaii Department of Education
P.O. Box 2360
Honolulu, HI 96804
808-586-3230
doe.k12.hi.us

Idaho Department of Education
650 West State Street
PO Box 83720
Boise, ID 83720-0027
208-332-6800
www.sde.state.id.us/Dept

Illinois Department of Education
100 W. Randolph, Suite 14-300
Chicago, IL 60601
312-814-2220
www.isbe.state.il.us

Indiana Department of Education
State House, Room 229
Indianapolis, IN 46204-2795
317-232-0808
www.ideanet.doe.state.il.us

Iowa Department of Education
Grimes State Office Building
Des Moines, IA 50319-0416
515-281-5294
www.state.ia.us/educate

Kansas Department of Education
120 SE 10th Avenue
Topeka, KS 66612-1182
785-296-3201
www.ksbe.state.ks.us

Kentucky Department of Education
500 Mero Street
Frankfort, KY 40601
502-564-4770
800-533-5372
www.kde.state.ky.us

Louisiana Higher Education and Teaching
626 N. 4th Street
P.O. Box 94064
Baton Rouge, LA 70804-9064
225-342-4411
877-453-2721
www.doe.state.la.us

Maine Division of Certification and Placement
Department of Education
23 State House Station
Augusta, ME 04333
207-624-6618
www.state.me.us/education/homepage.htm

Maryland State Department of Education
200 W. Baltimore Street
Baltimore, MD 21201
410-767-0100
www.msde.state.md.us

Massachusetts Department of Education
350 Main Street
Malden, MA 02148-5023
781-338-3000
www.doe.mass.edu

Michigan Department of Education
608 W. Allegan Street
Hannah Building
Lansing, MI 43933
517-373-3324
www.mde.state.mi.us

Minnesota Department of Children, Families, and Learning
1500 Highway 36 West
Roseville, MN 55113
651-582-8200
www.educ.state.mn.us

Mississippi Department of Education
Central High School
P.O. Box 771
359 North West Street
Jackson, MS 39205
601-359-3513
www.mde.k12.ms.us

Missouri Department of Elementary and Secondary Education
P.O. Box 480
Jefferson City, MO 65102
573-751-4212
www.mde.k12.ms.us

Montana Office of Public Instruction
P.O. Box 202501
Helena, MT 59620-2501
406-444-3150
www.opi.state.mt.us

Nebraska Department of Education
301 Centennial Mall South
Lincoln, NE 68509
402-471-2295
www.nde.state.ne.us

Nevada Department of Education
700 East Fifth Street
Carson City, NV 89701-5096
775-687-9200
www.nde.state.nv.us

New Hampshire Department of Education
101 Pleasant Street
Concord, NH 03301-3860
603-271-3494
www.ed.state.nh.us

New Jersey Department of Education
P.O. Box 500
100 Riverview Place
Trenton, NJ 08625-0500
609-292-4469
www.state.nj.us/education

New Mexico Department of Education
Licensure Unit
Education Building
300 Don Gaspar
Santa Fe, NM 87501-2786
505-827-6516
sde.state.nm.us

New York State Education Department
Education Building
89 Washington Avenue
Albany, NY 12234
518-474-5844
www.nysed.gov

North Carolina State Department of Public Instruction
301 N. Wilmington Street
Raleigh, NC 27601-2825
919-807-3300
www.dpi.state.nc.us

North Dakota Education Standards and Practices Board
600 E. Boulevard Avenue, Dept. 201
Floors 9, 10, & 11
Bismark, ND 58505-0440
701-328-2260
www.dpi.state.nd.us

Ohio Department of Education
Teacher Education and Certification and Professional Development
25 South Front Street
Columbus, OH 43215-4183
877-772-7771
www.ode.state.oh.us

Oklahoma State Department of Education
2500 N. Lincoln Boulevard
Oklahoma City, OK 73105-4599
405-521-3301
sde.state.ok.us/home

Oregon Department of Education
255 Capitol Street NE
Salem, OR 97310-0203
503-378-3569
www.ode.state.or.us

Pennsylvania Department of Education
333 Market Street
Harrisburg, PA 17126-0333
717-783-6788
www.pde.psu.edu

Rhode Island Department of Education
255 Westminster Street
Providence, RI 02903
401-222-4600
www.ridoe.net

South Carolina Department of Education
Rutledge Building
1429 Senate Street
Columbia, SC 29201
803-734-8815
www.sde.state.sc.us

South Dakota Department of Education
Kneip Building, 3rd Floor
700 Governors Drive
Pierre, SD 57501-2291
605-773-3134
www.state.sd.us/deca

Tennessee State Department of Education
Andrew Johnson Tower, 6th Floor
710 James Robertson Parkway
Nashville, TN 37243-0375
617-741-2731
www.state.tn.us/education

Texas Education Agency
William B. Travis Building
1701 N. Congress Avenue
Austin, TX 78701-1494
512-463-9734
www.tea.state.tx.us

Utah State Office of Education
250 East 500 South
Salt Lake City, UT 84111
801-538-7500
www.usoe.k12.ut.us

Vermont Department of Education
120 State Street
Montpelier, VT 05620-2501
802-828-3135
www.state.vt.us/educ

Virginia Department of Education
P.O. Box 2120
Richmond, VA 23218
800-292-3820
www.pen.k12.va.us

Washington Department of Education
Old Capitol Building
P.O. Box 47200
Olympia, WA 98504-7200
360-725-6000
www.k12.wa.us

West Virginia Department of Education
1900 Kanawha Boulevard East
Charleston, WV 25305
304-558-2681
wvde.state.wv.us

Wisconsin Department of Public Instruction
P.O. Box 7841
125 S. Webster Street
Madison, WI 53707
800-441-4563
www.dpi.state.wi.us

Wyoming Department of Education
2300 Capitol Avenue
Hathaway Building, 2nd Floor
Cheyenne, WY 82002-0050
307-777-7675
www.k12.wy.us

Appendix B

Print Resources

ACT EXAM GUIDES

ACT Assessment Success 2003. (New York: Petersons, 2002).

Bobrow, Jerry, et. al. *Cliffs Test Prep ACT Preparation Guide*. (Hoboken: Wiley, 2000).

Chesla, Elizabeth, Matic, Jelena, Grove, Melinda, and Hirsch, Nancy. *LearningExpress's ACT Assessment Success*. (New York: LearningExpress, 2003).

Domzalski, Shawn Michael. *Crash Course for the ACT: The Last-Minute Guide to Scoring High*. (New York: Princeton Review, 2000).

Ehrenhaft, George, et. al. *How to Prepare for the ACT*. (Hauppauge, NY: Barron's, 2001).

Getting into the ACT: Official Guide to the ACT Assessment. (New York: HBJ, 1997).

Kaplan ACT 2000 with CD-ROM. (New York: Kaplan, 2002).

Magliore, Kim, and Silver, Theodore. *Cracking the ACT*. (New York: Princeton Review, 2002).

Panic Plan for the ACT. (New York: Petersons, 2000).

AP EXAM GUIDES

Foglino, Paul. *Cracking the AP Chemistry Exam 2002–2003*. (New York: Princeton Review, 2002).

Kahn, David S. *Cracking the AP Calculus AC & BC Exams: 2002–2003*. (New York: Princeton Review, 2002).

Leduc, Steven A. *Cracking the AP Physics B & C Exams, 2002–2003*. (New York: Princeton Review, 2002).

McDuffie, Jerome. *REA's AP US History Test Prep with TESTware Software*. (Piscataway, NJ: Research and Education Association, 2001).

McEntarffer, Robert, and Weseley, Allyson. *How to Prepare for the AP Psychology: Advanced Placement Examination*. (Hauppauge, NY: Barron's, 2000).

Meltzer, Tom, and Hofheimer Bennett, Jean. *Cracking the AP U.S. History Exam, 2002–2003*. (New York: Princeton Review, 2002).

Pack, Philip E. *Cliffs AP Biology*. (Hoboken: Wiley, 2001).

Springer, Alice Gericke. *How to Prepare for the AP Spanish*. (Hauppauge, NY: Barron's, 2001).

Swovelin, Barbara V. *Cliffs AP English Language and Composition*. (Hoboken: Wiley, 2000).

ASVAB EXAM GUIDES

ASVAB, 2nd edition. (New York: LearningExpress, 2000).

ASVAB Core Review: Just What You Need to Get into the Military. (New York: LearningExpress, 1998).

Fogiel, M. *The Best Test Preparation for the ASVAB: Armed Services Vocational Aptitude Battery*. (Piscataway, NJ: Research and Education Association, 1998).

Green, Sharon Weiner, and Wolf, Ira K. *Pass Key to the ASVAB: Armed Services Vocational Aptitude Battery: With Intensive Review of: Arithmetic Reasoning, Math Knowledge, Word Knowledge*. (Hauppauge, NY: Barron's, 2000).

How to Prepare for the Armed Forces Test ASVAB: Armed Services Vocational Aptitude Battery. (Hauppauge, NY: Barron's, 2000).

Kiehl, Andy, Moss, Nicole, and Winn, David. *Cracking the ASVAB*. (New York: Princeton Review, 2002).

Ostrow, Scott A. *ASVAB: Armed Services Vocational Aptitude Battery: Everything You Need to Score High on the ASVAB*. (New York: Arco, 2001).

Vincent, Lynn. *ASVAB Success*. (New York: LearningExpress, 2001).

PSAT EXAM GUIDES

Green, Sharon Weiner, Wolf, Ira K., and Weiner, Mitchel. *How to Prepare for the PSAT/NMSQT: PSAT/National Merit Scholarship Qualifying Test*. (Hauppauge, NY: Barron's, 1999).

Kaplan Fast Track SAT & PSAT. (New York: Kaplan, 2001).

Robinson, Adam, and Rubenstein, Jeff. *Cracking the PSAT/NMSQT, 2003*. (New York: Princeton Review, 2002).

SAT & PSAT 2002. (New York: Kaplan, 2001).

SAT EXAM GUIDES

10 Real SATs. (College Entrance Examination Board, 2000).

Reed, C. Roebuck, and Antor, Maxwell. *LearningExpress's SAT Exam Success*. (New York: LearningExpress, 2003)

ARCO: Master the SAT 2003. (New York: Arco, 2002).

Bell, Robert A. *Quick Review for the SAT*. (Piscataway, NJ: Research and Education Association, 1994).

Berger, Larry, et. al. *Up Your Score: The Underground Guide to the SAT 2003–2004 Edition*. (New York: Workman, 2002).

Carris, Joan Davenport. *Panic Plan for the SAT*. (New York: Petersons, 2001).

Elliott, Joseph, and Elster, Charles Harrington. *Tooth and Nail: A Novel Approach to the New SAT*. (Orlando: Harcourt, 1994).

Green, Sharon Weiner, and Wolf, Ira K. *How to Prepare for the SAT I*. (Hauppauge, NY: Barron's, 2001).

Karelitz, Raymond. *The New SAT in 10 Easy Steps*. (Avon, MA: Adams Media Corporation, 1994).

Katzman, John, and Robinson, Adam. *Cracking the SAT with CD-Rom, 2003 Edition*. (New York: Random House, 2002).

Kleinman, Liza, and Steddin, Maureen. *SAT Success: The Only Test-Prep Guide with Bonus Software*. (New York: Petersons, 2002).

Martin, Sandra. *SAT Savvy: Last Minutes Tips and Strategies*. (Alexandria, VA: Octameron Associates, 1999).

Orton, Peter Z., and Rimal, Rajiv N. *30 Days to the SAT*. (New York: Petersons, 2001).

SAT & PSAT 2002. (New York: Kaplan, 2001).

Weber, Karl. *The Insider's Guide to the SAT*. (New York: Petersons, 2001).

Weber, Karl. *The Pocket Guide to the SAT*. (Orlando: Harcourt, 1985*)*.

GENERAL STUDY GUIDES

Fry, Ronald. *Ace Any Test*. (Franklin Lake, NJ: Career Press, 1996).

Huntley, Sara Beth, and Smethurst, Wood. *Study Power Workbook: Exercises in Study Skills to Improve Your Learning and Your Grades*. (Cambridge: Brookline Books, 1999).

Kornhauser, Arthur William. *How to Study: Suggestions for High School and College Students*. (Chicago: University of Chicago, 1993).

Luckie, William R., and Smethurst, Wood. *Study Power: Study Skills to Improve Your Learning and Your Grades*. (Cambridge: Brookline Books, 1997).

Meyers, Judith. *The Secrets of Taking Any Test, 2nd edition*. (New York: LearningExpress, 2000).

Semones, James. *Effective Study Skills: A Step-by-Step System for Achieving Student Success*. (Washington, DC: Thomson, 1991).

Wood, Gail. *How to Study, 2nd edition*. (New York: LearningExpress, 2000).

Online Resources

ACT EXAM WEBSITES

www.act.org—The official ACT exam website.

www.testprep.com/practicehdr.shtml—Provides practice tests for the ACT exam.

www.powerprep.com—Provides strategies, tutoring, software, diagnostic and online practice tests for the ACT exam.

www.review.com—Provides tutoring and test preparation for the ACT exam.

www.kaplan.com—Provides tutoring, test preparation, and general information for the ACT exam.

www.act-sat-prep.com—Provides practice exams and strategies for taking the ACT exam.

www.learnatest.com—Provides two complete practice tests for the ACT exam.

AP EXAM WEBSITES

www.collegeboard.com/ap/students—Provides AP exam information, answers for frequently asked questions, and an array of online practice exam materials.

www.learnatest.com—Provides online AP practice exams for biology, U.S. history, calculus, and English literature & Composition.

apcentral.collegeboard.com/homepage—The official AP exam site provides AP exam schedules, sample exam questions, and tips.

www.pahomeschoolers.com/courses/welcome.html—Provides online AP exam preparation specifically for homeschoolers.

ASVAB EXAM WEBSITES

www.dmde.osd.mil/asvab/CareerExploration Program/—The official ASVAB exam site.

www.todaysmilitary.com/explore_asvab.shtml—Comprehensive guide to the ASVAB exam that provides a detailed description of the exam, registration information, and sample questions.

www.4youonline.com/asvab—Provides online study guides and interactive online courses to help you prepare for the ASVAB exam.

www.petersons.com/testprepchannel/asvab_index.asp—Provides practice exams as well as tips and strategies for taking the ASVAB exam.

usmilitary.about.com/library/weekly/aa043001a.htm—Provides a detailed description of the ASVAB exam and its history, instructions for interpreting your score, and sample questions.

www.learnatest/com/military/home.cfm—Provides interactive practice exams and guides to help you prepare for the ASVAB exam.

SAT AND PSAT EXAMS WEBSITES

www.testprep.com/practicehdr.shtml—Provides practice tests for the SAT and PSAT exams.

www.powerprep.com—Provides strategies, tutoring, software, diagnostic and online practice tests for the SAT exam.

www.collegeboard.com—The official SAT exam site provides online test registration and test preparation for the SAT exam.

www.review.com—Provides tutoring and test preparation for the SAT and PSAT exams.

www.kaplan.com—Provides tutoring, test preparation, and general information for the SAT exam.

www.act-sat-prep.com—Provides online test registration, practice exams, and strategies for taking the SAT exam.

www.learnatest.com—Provides several online practice tests and an online course series to help you prepare for the SAT exam.

GENERAL WEBSITES

members.aol.com/TeacherNet/Study.html—Provides a comprehensive index of practice exams, study guides, and study aids for various college entrance exams, including the CLEP, AP, ACT, and SAT exams.

dmoz.org/Reference/Education/Products_and_Services/Test_Preparation—Provides test preparation materials, study guides, and study aids for various college entrance exams, including the ACT, PSAT, and SAT exams.

db.education-world.com/perl/browse?eat_id=978—Provides a comprehensive index of tutoring services, practice exams, study guides, and study aids for various college entrance exams, including the ACT, SAT, and AP exams.

www.teacheroz.com/college.htm—Provides study aids, strategies, and reference materials for the AP, SAT, and Regents exams.

www.attheu.com/admissions/test_prep/test_prep.asp—Provides tutoring, courses, test preparation software, practice exams, and test-taking tips and strategies for the PSAT, SAT, and AP exams.

www.learnatest.com—Provides practice exams for the ACT, ASVAB, AP, and SAT exams, and many more professional and academic tests.